How to Observe Children

Sheila Riddall-Leech

www.heinemann.co.uk

✓ Free online support
✓ Useful weblinks
✓ 24 hour online ordering

01865 888058

Inspiring generations

Heinemann Educational Publishers
Halley Court, Jordan Hill, Oxford OX2 8EJ
Part of Harcourt Education
Heinemann is the registered trademark of Harcourt Education Limited

Text © Sheila Riddall-Leech 2005
First published 2005
09 08 07 06 05
10 9 8 7 6 5 4 3
British Library Cataloguing in Publication Data is available from the British Library on request.
10-digit ISBN: 0 435401 86 6
13-digit ISBN: 978 0 435401 86 3

Typeset by Saxon Graphics Ltd, Derby
Printed by The Bath Press Ltd
Original illustrations © Harcourt Education Limited, 2005
Cover design by Wooden Ark Studio
Cover photo: © Photonica

Acknowledgements

Every effort has been made to contact copyright holders of material reproduced in this book. Any omissions will be rectified in subsequent printings if notice is given to the publishers.

Photo acknowledgements

Page 2: Harcourt Education Ltd/Jules Selmes; page 5: Harcourt Education Ltd/Jules Selmes; page 13: Harcourt Education Ltd/Jules Selmes; page 16: Harcourt Education Ltd/Jules Selmes; page 18: Harcourt Education Ltd/Jules Selmes; page 31: Harcourt Education Ltd/Tudor Photography; page 42: Harcourt Education Ltd/Jules Selmes; page 49: Harcourt Education Ltd/Tudor Photography; page 53: Corbis; page 60: Harcourt Education Ltd/Jules Selmes; page 66: Mother and baby picture library; page 69: Harcourt Education Ltd/Jules Selmes; page 77: Harcourt Education Ltd/Jules Selmes; page 81: Harcourt Education Ltd/Jules Selmes; page 85: Harcourt Education Ltd/Jules Selmes; page 88: Harcourt Education Ltd/Jules Selmes; page 94: Harcourt Education Ltd/Jules Selmes; page 99: Harcourt Education Ltd/Jules Selmes; page 106: Harcourt Education Ltd/Jules Selmes; page 110: Harcourt Education Ltd/Tudor Photography; page 114: Harcourt Education Ltd/Jules Selmes; page 119: Harcourt Education Ltd/Jules Selmes; page 128: Corbis.

Author acknowledgements

The author would like to thank everyone who has been involved in this book, from staff and children in a large number of settings to the editorial team at Heinemann.

Special mention to Peter for his continued love, support and encouragement and to two very special children Laura and Caroline.

The author and publisher are grateful to QCA (Enterprises) for permission to reproduce the KS1 and KS2 schemes of work for Speaking and the Curriculum 2000 Scientific Enquiry sample recording sheet.

Sheila Riddall-Leech
May 2005

Contents

Introduction

Spend time in any situation where there are children and you will inevitably find yourself watching them. This is a form of observation that is done almost unconsciously, and sometimes we even find ourselves observing and making decisions about the children without being fully aware that we are doing so.

Most childcare and education courses include observations and assessment of children as part of the syllabus. Some of these courses include observations in the assessment requirements. Observations form a vital part of the Foundation Stage Profile and underpin practice in the Birth to Three Matters Framework. So why is so much importance given to something that the majority of parents, childcare and education practitioners, as well as teachers and students, do almost instinctively?

This book aims to help practitioners understand the importance of observing and the difference that this skill can have on meeting children's needs. It is written in two sections. The first part of the book looks at why we observe children, what we can learn from observing, and how to observe effectively. The second part of the book links observations to research, theoretical perspectives and theories, and enables practitioners to plan appropriate activities that will meet children's individual needs. Observations should not be carried out and then 'made to fit' a theory or perspective, but used as a starting point to help the observer learn more about the child and their needs. Chapter five looks at ways in which the developmental norms can be used to support observational evidence in providing for children's developmental needs. Chapters six, seven and eight also consider the importance of observations to the Birth to Three Matters Framework, the Foundation Stage Curriculum, and the National Curriculum.

Throughout this book the reader is encouraged to find out more in order to increase their own knowledge and understanding about a topic. For example, repeated reference is made to the CD-ROM that is part of the Birth to Three Matters pack, but although an excellent source of information this is only one of many avenues that can be explored. Practitioners need to be reflective and open-minded, they should be aware of current research and differing views and perspectives. The Internet is an inexhaustible supply of information, but do not forget professional journals, books, television and newspapers, all of which are useful sources. This book addresses anti-discriminatory and anti-bias practice by constant reference to meeting individual needs and planning and providing appropriate activities and experiences for babies and children.

Part 1

The observation process

Chapter 1 Why observe children?

The quality of observations and subsequent assessment of children's development and learning depends very much on the skills of the individual practitioner. If observations are going to be worthwhile, meeting individual children's needs and providing information for the future planning of activities and experiences, they should consistently be of the highest possible quality. Practitioners should ensure that children make progress and that recognition is given to their achievements. To this end, observations are the key to quality provision.

In many childcare and education awards and qualifications, students are required to carry out several repeated observations following a set format or pattern. Some students have difficulty understanding why they are required to do so many observations, and also what to do with the information that they have recorded.

This chapter will consider:

◆ why observing and assessing children is important for the children themselves, the practitioners working with them and other professionals that have contact with the children

◆ what can be learned from observing children, including how to meet individual needs

◆ how to plan appropriate activities for children's progress and achievement

◆ how observations can help with professional development.

Why observing and assessing children is important

One of the fundamental purposes of observing children is to enable adults to gain greater understanding of their needs. All children have unique qualities. If we are to meet children's individual needs effectively it is essential that we recognise their differences and acknowledge that they have a right to be treated with respect.

Children want to share their achievements with the adults around them, be it successfully getting finger-foods into the mouth or painting a picture that represents a memorable event. Observing them can help us share their achievements and empathise with the child's positive feelings. However, children should never be put into situations that might cause them distress or could be deemed unethical.

Sharing achievements with children is an important part of the observation process

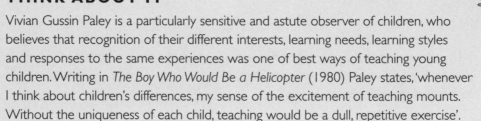

THINK ABOUT IT

Vivian Gussin Paley is a particularly sensitive and astute observer of children, who believes that recognition of their different interests, learning needs, learning styles and responses to the same experiences was one of best ways of teaching young children. Writing in *The Boy Who Would Be a Helicopter* (1980) Paley states, 'whenever I think about children's differences, my sense of the excitement of teaching mounts. Without the uniqueness of each child, teaching would be a dull, repetitive exercise'.

Without sensitive interpretation and analysis the information obtained from observing children is merely a description of what the observer has seen. To be of use it must inform our responses to children's needs, develop our understanding of children and ultimately benefit them.

The importance of observations for practitioners

Imagine driving a car down the road and becoming aware of a loud knocking noise coming from somewhere under the bonnet. What would you do?

◆ Turn the music up louder so that the noise can't be heard?

◆ Ignore it, and drive faster in the hope that it might stop?

◆ Pull over in a safe place, stop, and take a look under the bonnet?

◆ Phone a friend?

The same approach can be applied to children, in that choices can be made about what action to take. For example, whilst watching a group of children playing outside you become aware that one of them is not joining in the fun. So what do you do?

◆ Ignore the child – they look happy enough, so leave them alone?

◆ Go over and talk to the child to find out if they are all right?

◆ Tell another member of staff?

◆ Do something else?

It is hoped that the first point would not be the preferred choice, but the main thing to consider is that the child has been observed, and, as a result, it is possible to find out more about what they are doing and why they are doing it. A process has taken place: **observation**, **assessment** and **decision-making**. This process is the main reason why professionals, students, and parents observe – because they want to find out more about the children. Observations and assessments are key to increasing personal and individual knowledge and understanding of children.

Observations and the development of children

Observations can be used to understand more about the stages of a child's development. Health visitors and doctors regularly observe and assess children to check if there are any developmental issues. Both parents and healthcare professionals regard these routine checks as very important ways of making an early diagnosis of possible problems. For example, the Apgar score is a form of assessment based on observations made by a midwife at one, five and ten minutes after birth. It is a routine event within the delivery room and can be critical in detecting many developmental issues, such as if the baby will require special care. This is an activity not automatically associated with observations, but one that was initiated and developed through observation.

Social workers, speech therapists, educational psychologists, child psychologists and other professionals working with children all use observations as part of their work, so learning how to observe plays a key part in their training.

Observations and assessments

Observations and assessments are used to gather information about a child's progress. An observation on its own is like a photograph, it can only record what is happening at that specific point of time. As such, single observations are not enough for any professional to decide whether or not a child is making progress and developing skills.

For example, Standard Assessment Tests (SATs) are currently undertaken at 7, 11 and 14 years of age, a significant period of time (note that seven year-olds do not take SATs in Wales). The purpose of these tests is to collect information on a child's progress in key subject areas of the National Curriculum.

SATs are supported by observations, and it is usual practice for teachers to carry out frequent observations and assessments of the development of skills – one observation of a child is not enough to reach a conclusion. The child in question may simply be having a bad day, be tired, or be distracted by something else. However, a teacher might, over the period of a few weeks, make several observations of a child's reading ability, to check that the child is developing skills and making progress with reading.

The importance of observations for other professionals

A child may have contact with other professionals on many occasions and for a wide variety of reasons. For example, health visitors and doctors regularly carry out developmental and medical checks on children. Other professionals such as speech therapists, child psychiatrists, child psychologists, education psychologists, play therapists and inclusion officers may also carry out observations to assess and treat a child who has been referred to them. Sometimes other professionals will ask early years practitioners, teachers and adults, such as classroom assistants, to carry out specific observations or keep records in order to build up a more holistic view of the child. Special Education Needs Coordinators (SENCO) will carry out observations of children to support individual action, or compile and compare educational plans to assess targets that have been set for a child.

What can we learn from observing children?

Observing children is a skill that anyone can develop, but few people are natural observers. We often assume that most people who see what we see will interpret the information in the same way, but we all have a tendency to see what we are looking for and, furthermore, to only look for what we know about.

THINK ABOUT IT

Imagine that you and your colleagues are outside with a group of children. One person might see a group of children playing cooperatively, but another might think that one child has been on a tricycle for too long and is therefore not sharing. You might be aware of a child who is standing watching the others play, but not actually participating. All of you have spotted different things from the same situation, based on your previous knowledge of the children, as well as your own preconceptions, attitudes and influences.

The vast majority of people have to learn how to observe effectively. In other words, to keep an open mind, avoid preconceptions, remain focused, and record information in a systematic and logical way. However, at the same time a skilled observer will recognise their own unavoidable bias and make allowances for it.

Once we have learned effective observation skills we can use them in a variety of situations and circumstances. But what can be learned from observing children?

Firstly, observing children will help develop a greater awareness of children's individual needs. Practitioners and other professionals who have been working with children for a long time build up a wealth of knowledge based on their experiences with them. They can produce accurate and perceptive observations and assessments of children's learning and development, and plan appropriate activities as a result. However, there is a danger of becoming a 'stick-in-the-mud' with the view that one way which has previously worked will always work; such individuals may well undervalue the importance of observations in identifying children's needs. Sometimes a person who is relatively new to the observation process can make a very worthwhile contribution to the assessment of a child's needs by looking at an old problem through fresh eyes.

CASE STUDY

Emma is studying a Level 3 Childcare and Education course and has been placed in a nursery class of an Early Years Unit. She quickly learns the different characteristics of the children, such as who likes to play on the computer, who likes to play in the role-play area and so on. Emma asks the nursery teacher if she can spend time with Kyle on a one to one basis, whilst he is playing. She is aware that Kyle, aged three years and six months, rarely speaks to her or other children, but does follow simple instructions and is aware of what is going on. Kyle seems to prefer to play alone, and talks to himself.

Emma has made some significant observations and assessments regarding Kyle's communication and social skills, and his individual needs. She has also responded in a positive way towards Kyle. However, she has no written evidence that could be used in the future to plan appropriate activities for Kyle. Also, she does not know:

◆ if Kyle has reached a developmental milestone or norm appropriate to his age and stage of development
◆ why Kyle does not communicate with others
◆ if there is a cause for concern.

Emma is taking positive action regarding Kyle's activities and experiences without knowing very much about him. Is Emma right to meet Kyle's needs in this way, however well intentioned she may be, without having the full picture or any tangible evidence? On the other hand, however, Emma is making significant efforts to meet Kyle's needs and this should not be disregarded or devalued.

If early years professionals wish to develop a greater awareness of how to meet individual needs or promote development in a specific area it is necessary to follow the correct observation process. Using the case study on page 6 they should undertake a series of observations focusing on different aspects of Kyle's development. For example, an aim of one observation could be to consider Kyle's interactions with other children and adults over a period of time. Another aim could be to consider Kyle's ability to follow instructions, or to look at his concentration levels during story time, for example. These observations could provide evidence about Kyle's needs, his social and communication skills, and possibly identify if he is hearing spoken words accurately. They may also learn that 'self-talk' is a common feature of young children.

From the evidence gathered during an observation it is possible to make informed judgements about children and answer the following questions.

◆ Why is this child doing this?

◆ What strengths or areas for support have been identified?

◆ What should be done to meet this child's needs?

Informed judgements can be made in a variety of ways, including:

◆ discussing the evidence in confidence with another professional in order to get another viewpoint

◆ reading journals, texts, and researching on the Internet for information about children's development that is relevant to the evidence of the observation

◆ comparing the child's development with the broadly accepted 'norms' or developmental milestones.

Once some or all of these things have been done you will have developed a greater awareness of the child's needs. You will be in a stronger position from which to make assessments about their needs; and will be more able to suggest and plan activities and experiences that will enable them to progress. As mentioned earlier it is not possible to develop a greater awareness of children's needs based on one observation.

Consider the Foundation Stage Profile, which has been designed so that practitioners can build up their observations and assessments of children throughout an academic year. By using this method professionals can observe children's achievements throughout the year and plan appropriate activities. When children are observed in this way we begin to get an insight into their world. It can be a very empowering activity.

Look at the tracking observation below of a girl of three years and four months.

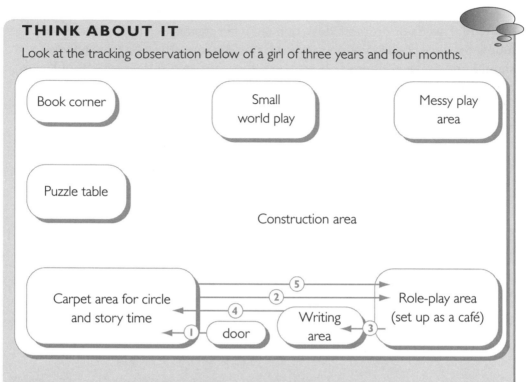

What does it tell you about this child's preferred activities?
What insight have you perhaps got into this child's world?

A quick look at the observation evidence tells you what this child's preferred activities are. She does not move around the room, staying quite close to the door. A sensitive observer might consider where the other adults were during the time of this observation and if this has any impact on the child's choice of activities. Furthermore, the observer might want to consider why this child does not move far away from the door, how she interacts with other children, who she plays with and what her needs are. However, the overall interpretation of this observation would depend on the original aim.

How to use observations to plan appropriate activities

Observations should not be stand-alone exercises produced to meet the assessment criteria of a particular course or curriculum requirement. The process of producing observations is not just an academic exercise. Any observation, regardless of the level of detail involved, should provide the data necessary to enable a professional to make balanced and informed decisions, such as the planning of specific activities to meet children's needs, or whether to seek professional help or advice.

To make sure that this can happen, it is vital that the observation evidence is:

1. Produced in a logical and systematic way.
2. Detailed.
3. Factual.
4. Accurate.
5. Non-judgemental and unbiased.
6. Used with permission.
7. Confidential.

The interpretation of observed evidence will be based on a sound footing if these criteria are followed and appropriate activities for children's progress and achievement can be planned and provided. More information about each point is outlined in the text below.

1. Produced in a logical and systematic way

Ask yourself:

- Is the evidence recorded in the exact order in which things happen?

- If you are using a pre-designed form, such as a checklist, have you completed it correctly, and is there evidence in all of the required areas?

- If you are writing the evidence, can someone else read your handwriting?

- Have you recorded the date and the start time?

- Have you indicated the length of time that you were observing for?

2. Detailed

Ask yourself:

- Are you focused on the aim of the observation?

- Have you written or recorded enough factual information to make your evidence clear to another person?

- Have you been in any way ambiguous in what you have recorded?

- Have you repeated any evidence, mistakenly thinking that you are adding detail?

3. Factual

Ask yourself:

◆ Have you recorded **exactly** what happened and what you saw, or have you recorded assumptions and what you thought had happened?

◆ If someone else read your evidence, would it be clear to them what you were observing?

4. Accurate

Ask yourself:

◆ Is your evidence factually accurate, and if so, are all the facts relevant to the case in point? Be careful when dealing with co-workers who could be offended by certain aspects of your findings.

◆ Have you got the order of events or the timings correct?

◆ Has your line manager or another professional signed your observation to confirm that it is an accurate and true record of events?

5. Non-judgemental and unbiased

Think about:

◆ Does your evidence contain statements that are biased or judgemental? If so, the evidence is neither accurate nor factual and should not be used to plan activities to meet the child's needs.

◆ Observations must be objective, even though this can sometimes be difficult when children are well known to the observer. It is essential that the description does not include statements containing value judgements that could influence the accuracy of the information.

6. Used with permission

Make sure:

◆ That before any observation is carried out permission has been given by the person in charge of the setting, for example a manager, a teacher or a headteacher.

◆ Before any observation is carried out the child's parents or primary carer must give permission. It is good practice for this permission to be in writing and kept with the child's records.

7. Confidential

It is essential that:

◆ Confidentiality is maintained at all times, which is an essential aspect of observing children.

◆ All records about children must be kept in a secure place and the information contained therein should not be shared unless there are specific legal reasons to do so, for example, when a child is deemed to be at risk.

◆ It is also essential to maintain anonymity of the children observed and the context in which they are observed. This is especially important if the observations are to be used as part of an assessed course requirement.

◆ If confidentiality and anonymity are not maintained the rights of the child concerned have been compromised and the practitioner has failed to meet that child's individual needs.

How observations can help with professional development

Anyone who works with children in any capacity has a duty of care to provide the best possible experience for them. In addition, professional development is also about being aware and responsive to the influences that could affect your judgements about children.

You must ensure that you keep up-to-date with modern views and thinking, and are aware of changes in legislation and statutory requirements, all of which aid your own professional development.

The very process of observing children will make you focus on the child and perhaps an aspect of development, or a skill. Hopefully you will start to ask yourself questions about what you have observed and seen. As you start trying to find answers to your questions you need to make sure that the information you are using is relevant and up-to-date.

THINK ABOUT IT

You may be concerned about what staff consider as the aggressive play-fighting of one child towards their peers, especially as your setting has a zero tolerance policy of war, weapon and superhero play. However, research by Penny Holland (2003) in her book 'We don't play with guns here', suggests that children who are imaginatively engaged and spend a substantial amount of time involved in imaginative play, including ostensibly 'aggressive' play have more developed social skills. So maybe the time has come for your setting to think again about its zero tolerance policy.

The influence of cultural perspectives

To a certain extent culture is an overused word, with many possible of meanings. In this instance it could be taken to mean a 'shared pattern of living' and, as such, is not static, but continually evolving and developing. Often, culture can include shared religious beliefs and the more common 'tokens' of culture that we all inherit, such as music and songs, stories, myths and legends, food and clothing.

However, as important, although possibly less obvious, is what is known as the 'shared total communication framework'. Within our cultural group we share not only the spoken and written words of our language, but also gestures and actions, tones of voice and facial expressions. When observing or communicating with members of other cultures we are more likely to notice differences in these actions. So it follows that if we want to be good at observing then we must also learn to be good at communicating. Smiling, eye contact, awareness of and sensitivity to personal space, touch and time concepts are key communication tools when observing children. For example, some African and Asian cultures regard eye contact as a sign of insolence, but to some western cultures a lack of eye contact is regarded with suspicion. Examples like this highlight the importance of gaining background knowledge of different cultures relating to the children in your care.

Language used

The observer's opinion about language use may well be influenced by attitudes and views in society on the status of different languages. Western languages such as French still seem to be held in higher regard by some than the languages of other communities, such as Urdu. In the same way the use of dialect can be undervalued according to individual opinion. For example, the accents of rural Aberdeenshire, Gloucestershire or Devon could be seen as preferable to the urban accents of Glasgow, Birmingham or Newcastle.

Physical appearance

Healthy, clean, alert children are commonly seen as being more appealing than unhealthy and unwashed children. Indeed, in order to survive a baby must be 'attractive' to the adult, so big eyes, a chubby face and soft skin are nature's way of ensuring that adults respond to the infant in an appropriate way. Anyone working with children may find themselves drawn to certain ones over others, although they will always try to maintain a fair and professional stance. Some children just simply do not have an air of attractiveness; they may seem dull, lifeless, unkempt, thin and miserable. This can influence the observer and may even affect their professionalism, and thus ultimately the care of the children involved.

THINK ABOUT IT

Some children look much older or much younger than they really are. How do you think this could affect or influence you during the observation process?

It is important to address gender roles within the care environment

Gender

Despite recruitment campaigns the professional world of caring and educating young children is still predominantly female. There are many reasons for this, including the level of pay, the perception of society towards the profession and the lack of promotion prospects. However, we do need to think about the message that the lack of male influence and lack of male role models gives to children at what is a developmentally crucial time. A female-dominated setting can influence young children's perception of gender roles through the resources selected, the activities and experiences provided, and also the attitude of the staff.

Referring back to the research of Penny Holland mentioned earlier in this chapter, studies have shown that a zero tolerance policy is almost exclusively directed towards boys (usually a small group). This can serve to reinforce passivity in girls, or a belief that girls are somehow 'nicer', which is just as dangerous. Note that a person's attitudes towards gender will have an impact on both their observed evidence and their interpretation of that evidence.

Bias

Your professional bias will be influenced by, amongst other things, your own upbringing, the environment in which you live and work, and your training. Everyone interprets observations in different ways and sees different reasons for actions.

What do you see in the picture on the right?

1. A happy child engaged in pretend play or an imaginative activity.
2. A dangerous situation – the child could fall and hurt themselves – they should be supervised more closely.
3. A child about to be destructive.

Your response will depend on your training and many other influences.

In conclusion, the process of observation provides proof of the quality of a practitioner's and a setting's provision. It presents the most reliable information about a child's progress and attainment. Observation should make practitioners reflective, open-minded and willing to learn. As such, the correct use of observation procedure is essential when considering the well-being of children.

Chapter 2 Preparing to observe

This chapter is designed to help you understand the preparation that is required for an effective observation. It will also look at ways of identifying and writing meaningful aims and objectives, which are a fundamental part of preparation. Some practitioners may refer to aims and rationales rather than aims and objectives. The meaning of 'rationale' is an underlying principle or a basis for something, but for the purposes of this book the term objective will be used.

In order to be factual, accurate and non-judgemental it is important that some form of logical and structured format is used rather than just a casual, almost instinctive, approach to observation. As such, consideration must be given to the information that should be included in every observation. This does not in any way fail to recognise the valuable and worthwhile observations many practitioners make that are not formally recorded, for example, on 'post-it' notes or in pocket notebooks.

This chapter will consider:

◆ developing aims and objectives

◆ planning

◆ format of observations including essential information

◆ confidentiality and obtaining permission.

Developing aims and objectives

Before carrying out an observation, it is important to develop and formulate its aims and objectives. This ensures that the observed information will be focused and can be effectively used to assess the child's development and plan appropriate activities and experiences.

An **aim** is a statement of what you intend to observe and what you would like to achieve. It is the overall purpose of the observation. Aims should be broad and can indicate the areas of development that you want to find out more about. For example, the aim of an observation could be:

To observe two children aged three years four months and three years five months playing with small-scale toys, focusing on language development.

Or:

To observe a baby aged five months three weeks interacting with their primary carer.

What might the observation objectives here be?

An objective is a statement of which particular skills or abilities you wish to observe or assess. It is a specific goal and is usually measurable. From the first example of an aim given on the previous page the objective could be:

To comment on and assess their language development, paying particular attention to vocabulary.

In this case the language could be noted and compared with language used in another activity in order to highlight situations where language is more freely used, as well as illustrating areas for development. This would be a form of assessment of their language development.

From the second example of an aim given on the previous page the objective could be:

To comment on and assess the methods used to interact – facial expressions, gestures, turn-taking.

In this case it would be possible to consider the theory of attachment and the development of bonds between the baby and its carer. (Attachment theory is discussed in chapter 4.)

You can view this from a different context. For example, if my aim is to win the lottery and this is what I would like to achieve, then my objective must be to remember to buy a ticket. This is therefore measurable – either I do remember to buy a ticket or I don't.

REMEMBER

Aims should be:
- child-centred
- focused
- precise
- unambiguous.

Objectives should:
- give a detailed reason for the observation
- be achievable and measurable
- be underpinned, either by developmental milestones or norms, or in another acceptable way such as theory or theoretical perspectives.

Look at the following suggested observations. For each one try to write an aim and an objective. You can use the Remember box above to help you.

1. An observation of a baby aged six months and two weeks during a routine care activity.
2. An observation of a child aged six years and three months during a science activity.
3. An observation of a group of six children aged between four years one month and four years eleven months playing outside.
4. An observation of a child at lunchtime, aged two years and eight months.
5. An observation of a child painting, aged three years and two months.
6. An observation of a child aged five years and one month looking at books.

Whilst the aims and objectives may focus on a particular aspect of the observation, the assessment may consider the whole observation and what else may emerge. This will avoid 'compartmentalising' or 'labelling' a child and should enable the observer to develop a holistic view of the child, linking all areas of development.

Planning observations

Observations need a well-organised approach and although this can be developed with practice, there is much that can be planned before the observation takes place. This does not mean that there is no place for spontaneous observations, but if the practitioner does not have a pen or pencil and something to write on immediately to hand, the spontaneity of the situation will be lost.

It is important to consider the following points before carrying out an observation.

Children often find it harder to concentrate in the afternoon

The time of day

Everyone has different responses to situations and experiences at different times of the day. Some people are referred to as 'night owls' because they are more lively later in the day than the 'larks' who are at their best early in the morning. Children can become tired towards the end of a busy day at school or pre-school session. Babies will often cry when they are tired and respond differently to their carers than when they are feeling refreshed. Choosing the time of day is very important and can make a significant difference to the overall effectiveness of an observation.

THINK ABOUT IT

Jackie wanted to observe the language development of a child aged two years and three months. Due to the pressure of work she did not find time to do this observation until after several children had gone home at around 4.30p.m. By this time the child concerned was in the book corner, listening to another adult read stories. She was sucking her thumb and curled up on a cushion but Jackie went ahead with her observation and tried to engage the child in conversation. They did not respond to Jackie's questioning and she had to abandon the attempt to observe this child.

Jackie should have known that the child was tired by this time of the day. Even if she did not know the child well, she should have been able to tell from the obvious physical signs of body position and thumb sucking that the child was tired. If this observation was really important then Jackie should have planned a slot in her work schedule to include it at a time when the child would have been responsive, for example at morning snack time.

The type of activity to observe

The type of activity to observe is not always implicit in the aim, for example, the aim could be to observe social skills with the objective being to assess if a group of four year olds had established friendships. It would be a good idea to carry out this observation when the children are playing freely, either indoors or outside, rather than when engaged in an activity which is adult-directed. This is because the adult-directed activity could be focusing upon developing specific skills, in which case opportunities for the children to interact with friends will be restricted.

The position of the observer within the setting

It is important that observations are always carried out discreetly and with sensitivity towards the observed child and those around them. Sometimes this is not as simple as it may appear. Children are naturally curious and will often ask what the adult is doing. Some people find that it is best to sit or stand somewhere

in the setting where they are partly out of sight. Also, some people do not start to record their observed data immediately, waiting for the children to be accustomed to their presence and lose interest in the adult's activities.

CASE STUDY

The staff of one nursery school all observe their key children each week, using a wide range of formats, activities and situations. The children are so used to seeing the adults engaged in observation activities that they no longer comment or ask what the adults are doing. Here, observation has become an accepted and valued part of the routine of the nursery for both staff and children.

Participating in observations

It can be difficult to be engaged in an activity with a child and observe them at the same time. Firstly, your focus may well be on the child, but your involvement may hinder the recording of data. Additionally, if you are engaged in an activity you may miss some vital information. For example, an observation of a baby at nappy changing time can provide much useful and valuable data about adult and child interactions, but while the observer cleans and wipes the baby's bottom, they may not be looking at the facial gestures of the baby. Such actions are an important part of social interactions. However, parents, carers, teachers and practitioners watch and observe children all the time; much of this is done instinctively and it would be highly unlikely if any of these observations were recorded. The results of these observations are often commented upon, such as 'look, he is trying to pull himself up!' or 'she wrote her name today without any help'. Observations such as these are often unplanned and spontaneous, but can be included into the overall organisation of the child's record of achievement. Informal comments made by parents can be very valuable and should not be disregarded.

Formatting observations to include essential information

It is good practice to develop a common format for observations. This ensures that all important and essential information is included. The following information is generally considered to be essential when writing up observations.

◆ **The date of the observation** – it is important to know when the observation was carried out in order to give a chronological approach to subsequent assessments.

◆ **The name of the observer** – it is important to identify who did the observation in case anything needs to be followed up.

◆ **The name by which the child is referred to in the observation** – this is the name or initials that you have used to identify the child throughout the observation. It is only necessary to record either a first or made-up name so that you respect the child's confidentiality.

◆ **The exact age and gender of the child** – the exact age of the child must be recorded, either in years and months or months and weeks, so that comparisons and assessments can be made of their development to accepted developmental norms or milestones.

◆ **The start time and finish time of the observation** – this is important because it allows you to consider how long a child may have spent doing an activity.

◆ **The method used** – including this will help you decide later if it was the best method to use in this situation.

◆ **The aim of the observation** – this should be a broad, focused statement about what you want to find out.

◆ **The objective** – this must be achievable and measurable.

◆ **Number of adults and children included** – the number of children and adults can be important additional information to include as it can provide an overview of the immediate context and may be useful when assessing the data.

◆ **A brief description of the setting** – to maintain confidentiality it is not necessary to name the setting, but it is useful to give a brief description of it because this puts the observations into context. It is also good practice to note the roles of any adults as this could affect the reactions and behaviour of the children.

◆ **A signature** – to confirm that the observation is a true record of what occurred. This gives the observation credibility and verifies its authenticity.

Many people find that having a proforma front sheet for this essential information is very useful and saves time. An example of such a proforma is given on page 22.

Using a proforma front sheet gives you a consistent and systematic approach, but does not give you all the information that an effective and meaningful observation should have.

NAME OF OBSERVER: A.N. Other **NAME OF CHILD:** J

DATE OF OBSERVATION: 25 06.04

EXACT AGE OF CHILD: Three years and five months

GENDER: Female

TIME OBSERVATION STARTED: 10:00a.m.

TIME OBSERVATION FINISHED: 10:10a.m.

METHOD USED: Written (or narrative)

NUMBER OF CHILDREN: 3 **NUMBER OF ADULTS:** 1

AIM OF OBSERVATION: to observe a child aged three years and five months playing in the water tray, focusing on physical development.

OBJECTIVE: To assess J's hand-eye coordination and comment on whether she has developed hand dominance.

BRIEF DESCRIPTION OF OBSERVATION SETTING:
J is playing with two other children at the water tray. The tray is in the messy play area of the pre-school room of a day nursery. There is one adult with the children.

OBSERVATION VERIFIED BY: A Person

The following written observation is complete and is designed to help you develop a greater understanding of how to construct and develop an observation. It has been adapted from an original piece of work submitted by a Level 3 student. It is **not** intended to be the perfect observation and, although you may identify areas where it could be improved, it does follow a logical format and include all essential information.

Other, more essential information for an observation can be recorded in a variety of ways. Sometimes the headings can be included, especially if the observations are to be assessed as part of a course requirement. Some experienced practitioners do not include all these headings within their observation sheets, but many do as a way in which to jog their memory. The most important information generally follows on from the proforma sheet and is outlined below.

◆ **Record of the actual observations or the description** – this is a factual record of exactly what happened during the observation. It should always be written in the present tense, regardless of which technique or method you use. You should try to concentrate on what the child does in relation to your aims and objective, because it is not possible to record absolutely everything that the child or children do. It is therefore very important that you stay focused and concentrate as best you can.

◆ **Conclusion** – this should be a summing up of what you recorded in the description. It should match what you stated in the objective.

◆ **Evaluation** – the evaluation should compare the evidence of your observation with developmental milestones/norms, or developmental theories and theorists if relevant. You can then make a judgement as to whether or not your views and opinions expressed in the conclusion are correct.

◆ **Recommendations** – the point of an observation is to provide evidence from which to plan and stage activities and experiences for the observed child that meet their individual needs. Recommendations should reinforce your evaluation, and endorse the aims and objective whilst taking into consideration the evidence of the observation and the conclusion.

If your observation is part of the assessment requirements for a course it is likely that you need to include the following headings, and it is also good practice for experienced practitioners to consider these points.

◆ **Personal learning** – as part of good practice it is useful to identify what you have gained and learned from carrying out this work. It can include developing your own understanding of child development, a greater awareness of the needs of children and an evaluation of the method of observation that was used: was it effective, and if not why not?

NOTE TO STUDENTS

Evaluation or analysis of theoretical perspectives is often required to meet the higher grading criteria of some awards. Some students doing observations find that at the start of their studies they may not have the in-depth background knowledge required to evaluate theoretical perspectives (i.e. identify strengths and weaknesses or plus and minus points). In the same way the skill of analysis, that of pulling something apart, thinking about each part and then making an overall comment can also be challenging at the start of a course. However, once gained it will provide a solid foundation upon which your knowledge and understanding of the subject can be built.

In the example given below the writer has attempted to evaluate the method of the observation used, they have considered the plus points and the minus points of the written method. However, they have not attempted to evaluate or analyse theoretical perspectives.

◆ **References and bibliography** – when you link an observation to a theory it is important to include references so that people reading your observations can work out what they are based on.

NOTE TO STUDENTS

Some courses specify a particular format with which to record references. The Harvard system tends to be the one most commonly used. When following the Harvard system you should include the author of the book/article or name of the website, the date it was published, the title of the book/article or website subject, and in the case of books and other publications, the publisher. This is an example of how you could do it:

Riddall-Leech, S. 2003. *Managing Children's Behaviour*. Oxford, Heinemann

The following example observation using a narrative or written method uses the information from the proforma front sheet and the headings described in the previous section. It is important that all of these factors work together because you need both sets of information for a complete and useful observation. Note that the text below is not purporting to be a perfect observation; it has some weaknesses that will be discussed at the end.

Description

J is standing by the sand tray watching two other children playing with a range of buckets, containers and plastic spades. 'Can I play too?' J asks the others, one child nods in reply so J rolls up the sleeve on her left arm, then the sleeve on her right arm and moves towards the sand tray. She positions herself opposite the two other children She reaches down and, using her right hand picks up a plastic bucket, which she puts down on the floor by her right foot, she then leans over and picks up a plastic spade with her left hand. She bends down, still holding the spade in her left hand and picks up the bucket with her right hand then places it back in the sand tray.

'What are you making?' she asks.

'We are making a castle to hide the animals in,' replies one child.

'Why don't you fill your bucket up and put the sand on top of the big pile?' says the adult.

J looks at the adult and nods, 'OK' she says.

J starts to dig in the sand with the spade, using her right hand and a palmar grasp she puts the first spadeful in the bucket. The sand does not go into the bucket which falls over and sand spills out. 'Oh dear,' says J. She puts the spade down in the tray and using both hands straightens the bucket. She picks up the spade with her left hand and then transfers it to her right. J puts her left hand around the bucket and digs in the sand again using her right hand and a palmar grasp. She puts the sand in the bucket. J digs again with the spade and, still holding the bucket, transfers sand into the bucket. She repeats this twice.

'This is hard work' she says to the adult.

'Is it?' replies the adult,' but you are doing very well, your bucket is nearly full.

J turns to the child standing next to her, 'You've got more sand than me,' she says.

The child looks at J and says, 'well I was here first'.

'J, why don't you put your bucket of sand on the pile?' says the adult.

'OK,' says J and puts the spade down in the sand. Using both hands around the bucket she lifts it up and stretches over to the pile of sand. J bites her bottom lip and looks at the pile and then at her bucket. Using both hands she slowly tips the bucket over and smiles as the sand falls out on to the pile. With her right hand J puts the empty bucket back in the sand tray.

'Look,' she says to the adult, 'there's something in the sand.' Using her right hand J moves her fingers over the surface of the sand and with a pincer grasp carefully picks up a small stone. J puts the stone into the palm of her left hand and using her right first finger carefully turns it over. 'It's shiny,' she says looking at the adult. 'We could put it on the shelf,' says the adult. J nods and walks over to the shelf, she stands on tiptoes and picks up the stone from her left palm with the thumb and first finger of her right hand. She places it on the shelf and then comes back to the sand tray. J starts to push down the sleeves of her left arm with her right hand, 'I don't want to play here anymore,' she says. 'That's OK,' says the adult, it is tidy-up time, so why don't you go and get the dustpan and brush so that we can sweep up the sand.' J nods and walks over to the shelf where the dustpan and brush are kept. She reaches out with both hands and grasps the dustpan and brush. She takes these over to the sand tray and puts them on the floor. With her right hand she picks up the brush. J bends down and begins to sweep with big arm movements. She is biting her bottom lip as she is doing this. She sweeps the sand towards the dustpan. She stops sweeping and reaches across with her left hand to pick up the dustpan. Using smaller movements than before J sweeps the sand into a small pile, and with the brush pushes it into the dustpan. 'Look, it's all tidy now,' she says to the adult. 'Thank you,' says the adult,' You've done a really good job.' J takes the dustpan and brush back to the shelf and then goes to sit on the carpet with the other children.

Conclusion

From the observation it can be seen that J tends to use her right hand more than her left, especially when she is doing quite controlled movements, such as using the spade. Although she used both hands to steady and straighten the bucket and to give more control when emptying the sand J does appear to have right hand dominance, as shown when she picked up the spade with her left hand and transferred it to her right hand again when picking up the small stone.

J did have some minor difficulties in transferring the sand from the spade into the bucket but was able to work out for herself a way to do this successfully. She used her left hand to steady the bucket and her right hand to fill the bucket. This again suggests that J has right hand dominance.

J showed good hand-eye coordination when she picked up the small stone and also when filling the bucket with sand. J also showed good hand-eye coordination when she sweeped up the sand at the end of the observation. J's facial expressions and body language, such as biting her bottom lip, suggest concentration when doing movements that require good hand-eye coordination. J bit her bottom lip on two occasions – once when transferring a bucket of sand on the pile and again when sweeping up the sand. This could indicate that she is not very confident when doing controlled small movements that require good hand-eye coordination, or that she is trying very hard.

Evaluation

J does appear to be functioning within the normal limits for her age. It is stated in Diploma in Childcare and Education (Tassoni et al, 2002, pp. 168) that children of two years begin to use their preferred hand. At three years and five months J clearly meets this developmental norm as she does use her preferred right hand more than the left hand. However, J does not manage to transfer the sand without spilling it and Tassoni et al state that children of three should be able to use a tool, such as a spade, without spilling. I am aware that J does not often choose to play in the sand area and it could be that she has not had very much opportunity to practice using a spade to transfer sand, or that she is uncertain and may need encouragement from an adult or her peers.

J can pick up small objects – using her thumb and first finger to pick up the small stone meets the expected developmental milestone for her age. This reinforces my view that she is operating within the usual boundaries for her age.

Recommendations

As previously stated J does not often play in the sand tray, so she could be encouraged to play there more often, perhaps with the support of an adult, and using a range of different tools. This could help her to develop her hand-eye coordination skills. Activities such as threading beads, pasta and buttons on to string, wool and laces will also help develop J's skills.

Personal learning

From this observation I have learned that J meets the developmental milestones that are appropriate for her age. I have also found out a lot more about fine motor skills through reading and this will help me plan appropriate activities for J that will meet her individual needs, hopefully enabling her to progress and develop her skills.

I used a written method for this observation, which I find quite difficult to do, as I am very aware that I could miss some important evidence whilst writing notes. I find it difficult to observe, write legibly and be aware of what is happening. However, I do not think that other methods of observation would have been any more effective, because this was an unstructured spontaneous activity. Many other methods, such as time samples and checklists require advance planning and proforma charts, and so cannot be used for unstructured and spontaneous observations. I think that despite the disadvantages of the written method it was the best to use for this observation.

I am also now more aware of different theories and perspectives of how children develop and learn. As I progress in my learning I hope that I will be able to form critical evaluations of these theories based on personal research and actual observations of the children that I am working with.

References and bibliography

Meggitt C. &, Sunderland G. 2000. Child Development, An Illustrated Guide. Oxford, Heinemann

Tassoni P. et al, 2002. Diploma in Childcare and Education. Oxford, Heinemann

Points to think about from this observation

◆ The writer has focused on fine motor skills in the conclusion, evaluation and personal learning sections of the observation. Whilst it could be argued that the writer has remained focused on the aim and objective, no consideration has been given to any other information that was evident in the description. Some of this information could have been richly informative. The description says a great deal about adult intervention, the child's use of language and the adult's support of the play.

◆ The recommendations suggest activities that the writer considers appropriate for this child, but does not say why. Is it considered that the child's skills need developing or extending? Again, no reference is made to other aspects of the observation.

◆ In the personal learning section the writer states that some observations such as time samples require a proforma, this is not necessarily correct as many practitioners use 'post-it' notes very effectively. Students may use a proforma for time and event samples but this is not a requirement of these methods.

◆ The writer comments about personal difficulties writing and observing at the same time. Whilst this is acknowledged as a difficulty for many observers, it is worth remembering that it is sometimes better to observe and then write the notes up later.

◆ The writer states that they have gained more awareness of different theories and perspectives, but do not state which ones. As this observation has focused exclusively on fine motor skills, it might have been reasonable to expect some discussion and reference to researchers such as Mary Sheridan (1975).

Confidentiality and obtaining permission

Confidentiality is an essential aspect of observing children. All records about children must be kept in a secure place and the information contained therein should not be shared with anyone. It is also essential to maintain the anonymity of the children observed and the context in which they are observed. This is especially important if the observations are to be used as part of an assessed course requirement. If confidentiality and anonymity are not maintained the rights of the child concerned have been compromised and the practitioner has failed to meet that child's individual needs. Information about a child should not normally be shared with anyone other than their parents or legal guardians, unless of course there are child protection issues. A sure test of confidentiality is whether another person could identify the child and the setting by reading the observation.

Many practitioners refer to the child by the initial of their first name, or as child A, or sometimes as TC (Target Child). Similarly, it is not necessary to name the setting, it is sufficient to describe it, for example, the toddler room of a day nursery, the quiet corner of a nursery class attached to a large inner city primary school, or a community hall in a rural market town.

When planning to carry out an observation it is necessary to obtain permission from the child's parents. It is good practice for this to be in writing and can be included in the admissions procedures of settings and retained in the child's file. Students should obtain permission from the setting supervisor, headteacher, class teacher or other appropriate practitioner.

Involving parents and carers in the observation process

Parents are the first educators of their children and as such have a wealth of information and knowledge about the child. Practitioners can get to know a child very well, but parents are the real experts when it comes to knowing about their child, yet many parents are unwittingly made to feel inadequate when discussing their child's attainment and progress. This can be very true for parents who do not use English as a first language. Involving parents in the observation process does not have to be difficult; and asking parents about a child's likes, dislikes, preferred activities and friends is an excellent starting point. Many settings invite parents and carers to contribute on a regular basis to a child's profile or record of achievement, or to record information about the child in the home. This can be carried out once a week, or even once every term. All of this information can inform and contribute to the observation process.

Chapter 3 Observation techniques

Get too close to children and you can interrupt what you are trying to observe

As stated in earlier chapters, observation requires a structure, a plan, or a format, all of which takes practice in order to perfect. There are many different formats or techniques in which to record an observation. However, no single technique is perfect and it is important that you are aware of the strengths and relative limitations of each. Skilled observers will be able evaluate the different techniques available and will be able to successfully select the most appropriate format for the observed situation and circumstance.

Using a range of different techniques when observing children will help you develop your own professional skills and become a more meticulous practitioner. It is good practice to use a range of different techniques over a period of time when observing a child, as this will help you to build up a more holistic picture. This is because some techniques lend themselves more to certain aspects of development. For example, a checklist might be a more effective way of recording specific physical skills than a written or narrative account.

This chapter will consider:

◆ different techniques or formats when observing children and recording the evidence

◆ the pros and cons of each technique

◆ the level of detail that is necessary for effective and sensitive conclusions and recommendations to be made.

Brief descriptions of techniques

There are many different techniques or formats for writing observations. Usually professionals refer to four main categories of observation techniques:

1. Written/narrative.

2. Checklists.

3. Diagrammatic.

4. Sampling.

The following descriptions are intended to give a brief overview of some of the most common techniques, but it should be remembered that it is necessary to practise each technique in order to make the best use of the information collected and be able to meet all children's individual needs.

1. Written/narrative

This category can include:

◆ structured recording of a pre-planned activity or task

◆ unstructured, spontaneous recordings

◆ child study

◆ diaries, sometimes called individual child development diaries

◆ snapshots.

These techniques are a way of collecting open data and can be used in both structured and unstructured situations. They can be used to collect information over a short space of time and should be written in the present tense, so that they read like a running commentary on what the child actually did. An example of an unstructured written technique can be found in the previous chapter on page 24. In order to do a written/narrative observation you must position yourself so that you can observe the child or children unobtrusively and not become involved in the activities. Many people find that this technique is the one they use the most.

Structured observations

For this technique you decide on a specific skill or developmental norm to assess and set up a specific activity, for example you might want to find out if a child of three years and six months can cut out pictures from a magazine using scissors. The objective of the observation could be to assess the child's hand-eye coordination, control, and fine motor skills when using scissors. In this case you would plan an activity with scissors and a number of magazines available and watch how the child carried out the task.

Pros

◆ You are focused on one specific activity.

◆ You can acquire a lot of data about the child and that specific skill.

Cons

◆ It is a contrived situation so the child might not behave as they would usually do, thus giving you inaccurate data about their abilities and skills.

◆ Can be limited in the data collected for the above reason.

Child study

A child study is usually a series of observations undertaken over a period of time, six months for example. It can build up a holistic picture of a particular child and different observation techniques, as well as written methods, can be used. It can also include photographs, with parental/carer's permission, and, if appropriate, examples of the child's work.

Pros

◆ Builds up a detailed and holistic picture of a child's progress and achievements.

◆ Can be used for comparisons in the future.

◆ Can be a positive record of a particular time in a child's life.

Cons

◆ Must be sustained over a period of time and this can sometimes be difficult to do because of staffing difficulties and other changes in circumstances.

Diaries, or individual child development diaries

Many settings use a form of diary to provide a valuable link between the setting and the child's home. They can help parents to feel involved in the assessment of their child and show that the childcare worker respects and values the partnership with, and the contribution of, parents and carers. With younger children and babies, diaries can record essential daily information for both parents and carers, such as what the child ate during the day, how much sleep they had, how many changes of nappy, and what activities they were involved in. For older children a diary could record social interactions, behaviour and academic progress. Parents and carers are often encouraged to write in the diary too, and can record information such as how the child passed the night, any concerns or achievements that have happened, or places that the child has visited during a weekend.

Pros

◆ Provides an essential and valuable link between home and the setting/school.

◆ Allows parents and carers to be involved in the assessment process of their child.

◆ Builds up a complete picture of the child because children can react and behave differently at home than in a school or day care setting.

Cons

◆ Must be regularly maintained by both the parent/carer and the school/setting.

◆ Can get lost between the two different places.

◆ Parents/carers may not agree with your assessment of their child so you must choose your words carefully – avoid making judgements without having all of the facts and do not make stereotypical statements.

Snapshots

A snapshot observation is exactly what the word implies, an instant 'picture' at one specific time. It is a flexible technique and can be used either to look at one specific child, a group, or to assess planned activities in the room. For example, you might want to assess how resources are being used and so record what children are doing at one specific moment on a chart, or in a written description, or even by photograph (with parental permission).

Pros

◆ Only need something to write on and something to write with.

◆ Can be spontaneous, does not always need to be planned.

◆ Provide open data that can be evaluated later.

- Can be used for both individual and group observations.

- Can be used for both structured and unstructured (naturalistic) observations.

Cons

- Can only realistically be used to record data over a very short space of time.

- It can be difficult to remain focused as children may ask you what you are doing. This should not, however, be a problem if children are used to seeing observations being carried out.

- You might miss something as you write down your observations.

- The notes of the observation need to be written up quickly afterwards or else you may forget information.

2. Checklists

This category can include:

- pre-coded charts

- portage records (portage is a home teaching service, usually for pre-school children who have a variety of conditions such as Down's syndrome or learning difficulties)

- checklists for partnerships or local education authorities (some partnerships and LEAs have developed recording systems that start when a child begins nursery education and are continued throughout their school life, thus providing a common format and consistency between settings).

The checklist technique is frequently used in schools and pre-school settings to record children's progress. Like the written technique it is also widely used by childcare professionals. Some local authorities provide proforma checklists that are used by all settings in the area. Health visitors and other professionals, such as portage workers, can also use checklists to check developmental progress. They are quick and easy to use and can be used over a period of time. They can be used for structured activities or completed during the normal course of events in the setting. Checklists can be used to record the development of one child or to compare the development of a group of children. An example of a section within a checklist for recording the achievements of one child is given in the table at the top of the next page.

Name:	Date:		
Date of birth (or exact age):	Name of observer:		
By five years	Yes	No	Sometimes
Can dress independently			
Can use appropriate eating utensils competently			
Can stand on one foot for 10 seconds			
Can ride a bike without stabilisers			
Can hop on each foot			

Pros

◆ Quick and easy to use.

◆ Can be used with either groups or on an individual basis for purposes of comparing levels of development.

◆ Can be repeated at a later date to check progress.

◆ Can be completed over a period of time (provided that the observer records the date each time they add something).

Cons

◆ Only records what a child did, not how they did it and, as such, is closed data.

◆ Often limited to one aspect of development.

◆ Limited data or information is recorded – the child might be able do more than is suggested by the information.

◆ The checklist must be prepared in advance, so planning is required (although checklists can be photocopied).

Comparative checklists

A comparative observation is usually used to compare or evaluate two children of the same age at the same time. It can also be used to compare and evaluate one child's achievements and/or skill level on two different occasions. In this case the first observation can be used as a baseline on which to build achievements. This is especially important when assessing children with special or additional needs. Comparative observations are often recorded as checklists, as in the example given in the table at the top of the next page, although they can sometimes be recorded as written observations.

Name of observer: Physical development	Baby A Age: Date:	Baby B Age: Date:
If lying on their back can roll over		
If lying on stomach can lift head and chest, supporting themselves on their arms and hands		
Will reach and grab an offered small toy		
Use palmar grasp to pass an object form one hand to the other		

Pros

- Can record a lot of data in the course of one observation.

- Simple and easy to use.

- Can be used with groups for purposes of comparing levels of development, or for one child to check progress at a later date.

- Can be completed over a period of time (provided that the observer records the date each time they add something).

Cons

- Only records closed data and does not give any indication of how the child performed the task.

- Needs to be pre-planned and therefore cannot be spontaneous.

- Does bring into question the value of comparing the achievements of children with one another. It could be suggested that we should be concerned with meeting *individual* needs, rather than comparing achievements.

3. Diagrammatic

This category can include:

- pie charts

- bar charts

- sociograms

- flow charts.

Pie and bar charts

These are diagrammatic and pictorial representations of the information gathered and both can be used to record results of an observation of a large group or whole class. For example, you might want to know how children in a class of 30 manage to use a physical skill such as kicking a ball at a target. These techniques can also be used to record information such as aspects of care in a baby's day, like how much time they spend feeding, sleeping, awake, playing etc. Pie and bar charts can be produced on a PC, and are often created in Microsoft Excel. Examples of both a pie chart and a bar chart are shown below.

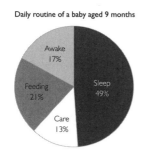

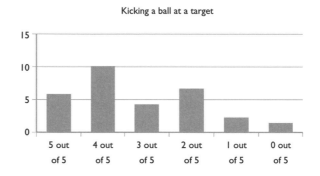

An example of a pie chart   An example of a bar chart

The pie chart (on the left above) represents 24 hours, and each section shows the number of hours that the baby is engaged in the specified activity expressed as a percentage of the whole day.

The numbers on the left-hand side of the bar chart (which is on the right above) indicate the number of children involved in the activity. For example, six children were able to kick a ball at a target on five out of five occasions; similarly, one child was not able to kick the ball at a target.

Pros

◆ Pie charts can cover any period of time or amount.

◆ Bar charts can record information about several children.

◆ Easy to read and interpret.

Cons

◆ May require good ICT skills on the part of the observer.

◆ Not everyone finds it easy to interpret data that is presented in a pictorial or diagrammatic format, so this technique may need some written commentary to accompany it.

◆ Needs to have a clear purpose and outcome.

Sociograms

Some people think that a sociogram is not a true observation, as it does not record behaviour or activities. The data from a sociogram can be used to assess social groupings or interactions, and the interpretation of that data can be used to suggest possible reasons why a child chooses to associate with certain children. The data is usually recorded on a pre-planned chart, but some successful sociograms have been developed using children's drawings of their friends. An example of a sociogram is given below. In this example children were asked to name or draw three other children that they most enjoyed associating, working or playing alongside. However, children can be quite unpredictable in their choice of friends and may choose a child, for example, who has recently invited them to a special outing, but may not choose that child to work alongside very often. They could even choose someone that they are afraid of.

Name	Friend	Friend	Friend
Sasha	Daisy	Amir	Annabelle
Amir	George	Daniel	Tariq
George	Amir	Daniel	Tariq
Daisy	Sasha	Jessica	Annabelle
Daniel	George	Tariq	Amir
Annabelle	Sasha	Daisy	Jessica
Charlie	Annabelle	George	Tariq
Jessica	Annabelle	Daisy	Sasha
Tariq	Amir	Annabelle	George

From this chart several deductions can be made, such as the most popular child, least popular child, same sex friendships and so on, but care must be taken when making these assumptions. On the chart above nobody picked Charlie, does this mean that Charlie is not a popular child, or maybe he was not in the room when the other children were being asked so they simply did not think to include him.

Pros

◆ A straightforward technique to use.

◆ Effective for looking at quite large groups of children.

Cons

◆ Cannot be done spontaneously, needs to be pre-planned.

◆ Relies on the views of the children at that particular time.

◆ Can be open to misinterpretation, so care and thought must be given to the interpretation of the data.

Flow charts

Flow charts can be used to record social interactions between small groups of children, or to track a child's movements around a room showing when they became involved with certain activities. In the latter case this is usually carried out over a morning, afternoon or whole day session. Examples of both are given below.

Example 1 – interactions of a small group

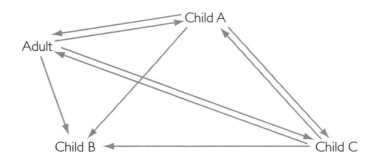

The arrows indicate the direction of the social interaction, so the adult communicates to all of the children, children A and C respond to the adult and to each other, but child B does not respond to anyone.

Example 2 – a single child's actions

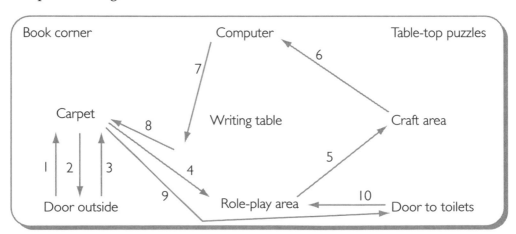

If the arrows track the movements of a child over morning session, starting with the one at the door, it can be seen that this child does not go to the activities in the book corner, writing table or the table-top puzzles. Therefore, conclusions can be drawn about the child's preferences, the provision of the activities, or even the role of the adult, although this last source of information is not recorded.

Pros

◆ Can be useful to assess the provision of activities in relation to a child's needs.

◆ Provides a full picture of the child's movements.

Cons

◆ Can get very untidy and therefore may be difficult to interpret.

◆ Uses closed data.

◆ Needs to be pre-planned on a specifically drawn plan and so is not spontaneous.

THINK ABOUT IT

The word 'spontaneous' usually refers to something that is done on the spur of the moment, being unprompted and natural. However, spontaneous observations can take place with careful pre-planning, for example, plans can be photocopied and made ready before observation sessions. Spontaneous observations can also be planned in the sense that a whole staff team can work on them over a period of time, showing how, by whom, and when observations will be carried out. This planning ensures that all children are observed more than once.

4. Sampling

This category can include:

◆ target child

◆ time sampling

◆ event sampling.

Target child

A target child observation focuses on one child and is usually recorded on a prepared chart using codes, for example, TC representing the target child, A for adult, and C for another child. In addition to these codes there can also be codes for describing the activities, such as Man for manipulative play, Pre for pretend play, and Dom for domestic activities such as hand washing. These are just a few examples – there can be many more and there are also codes to describe the social groups of the child, such as Sol for solitary play, SG for small group, and Pr for pair. The observation is usually recorded over a period of 10 minutes. An example of part of a target child observation is given on page 43.

A target child observation focuses on one child

Child's name: Jessica   **Gender:** Female

Age: 4 yrs and 6 months   **Date:** 31.03.2004

Time	Activity	Language	Task	Social group
1 minute	TC is threading beads onto a lace	None, TC hums to herself	Man	Sol
2 minutes	Reaches out to get more beads	TC → A asks for help in reaching the bead box	Man	A + TC
3 minutes	Continues to thread beads as another two children come to the table	TC → A + C tells them what she is making. A responds positively.	Man	SG
4 minutes	TC puts lace around her neck and tries to fasten it to make a necklace	A → TC asks if she thinks that it is long enough. TC nods. TC → A asks adult to fasten the lace	Man	SG
5 minutes	TC moves away from the table and goes to wash her hands for snack time	A tells all children that it is tidy up time	Dom	Sol

Pros

◆ Can be used for a range of different purposes, such as activities over a specific period of time, social interactions, language and communication.

◆ Is relatively clear and easy to use.

◆ Helps you focus on language, social interactions and activities of the child being observed.

Cons

◆ The observer does need to be familiar with the codes and needs good concentration skills.

◆ The information or data can be limited, but is not closed.

◆ Must be pre-planned and use a specially prepared chart, therefore cannot be used for spontaneous observations.

Time sampling

Time sampling can be used to record an individual or group of children. Recording is not continuous and is carried out at regular intervals, such as every 15 minutes throughout the day or session as appropriate. Time samples can be used to look at a child's specific activity or behaviour, and can be recorded on a prepared chart or produced as a written description. Below are examples of both.

Example 1 – prepared chart

Time	Activity	Comment
9:00a.m.	Arrives in classroom	Jake holds tightly onto his Mum's coat and does not reply when adult speaks to him. Follows instruction to hang up his coat. Starts to cry as Mum tells him she is leaving. Mum leaves and Jake runs to the window to watch her. Does not speak to the adult when she approaches him
9:15a.m.	Sitting on the carpet	Jake is still crying quietly but nods, avoiding eye contact, when the adult calls his name on the register
9:30a.m.	Writing table with a small group	Jake is with three other children sitting at the writing table. They are writing shopping lists for the trip to the shops tomorrow. One child asks Jake to pass her the eraser, he stretches across with his right hand and gives the eraser to the child, but does not speak and again avoids eye contact
9:45a.m.	Book corner	Jake is in the book corner on his own. The adult asks him if he would like to read a story with her. He puts his head down and shakes it to say no

Example 2 – written description

10:00a.m.	Sitting on the carpet looking at adult.
10:05a.m.	Concentrating on the story being read to the group.
10:10a.m.	Has her right hand up to answer a question about the story.
10:15a.m.	Is poking the child in front with her right index finger.
10:20a.m.	Adult moves her to a different place on the carpet.
10:25a.m.	Has her right hand up again to answer a question about the story. Adult asks child and she responds.

Pros

◆ Observations can be recorded over a long period of time.

◆ Open data is collected.

◆ Simple and easy to record.

◆ Can be used for individuals and groups of children.

Cons

◆ Can forget to record data at the correct time, so good timekeeping skills are needed.

◆ You may need to involve other adults if the recording is over more than one day or session

◆ You may not record something significant that the child does if it occurs outside of your timed recorded samples.

Event sampling

Event samples are similar to time samples but data is not recorded at fixed times. The frequency of the event determines the amount of information gathered. This observation technique is often used when there are concerns about a child, such as behaviour or emotional difficulties. However, this technique can also be used to record other events, such as how frequently a young child uses a comforter. This data is usually recorded on a chart, such as the example at the top of page 46, but the way the chart is set out will depend on the information required to meet the aim of the observation.

Event	Date and time	Situation	Comment
1	02.04.04 7:45a.m.	Arrives with Dad at nursery	Has comforter in mouth as Dad hands Kylie to her key worker
2	02.04.04 9:00a.m.	On the carpet playing with key worker	Kylie has her comforter in her hand. 'Can I have that?' asks the adult. Kylie shakes her head and puts the comforter in her mouth
3	02.04.04 9:30a.m.	In the rest room	Kylie has her comforter in her mouth as the key worker lays her down
4	02.04.04 9:50a.m.	In the rest room	The key worker takes the comforter out of Kylie's mouth. She immediately wakes up and starts to cry

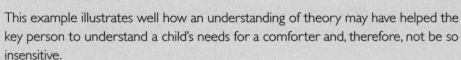

THINK ABOUT IT

This example illustrates well how an understanding of theory may have helped the key person to understand a child's needs for a comforter and, therefore, not be so insensitive.

Pros

◆ It is simple and easy to use.

◆ Open data is collected.

◆ Builds up a picture of a specific behaviour or concern.

Cons

◆ Needs a prepared chart and therefore cannot be spontaneous.

◆ May require input from other adults.

It must be remembered that regardless of which technique you use to record your data you must always provide the same essential information (described in chapter 2). Whether you record the information on a chart or diagram, or as description/narrative, you still need to identify the exact age of the child, your aims, and your objective. Once all this information has been gathered you will still need to think carefully about the conclusion you draw and any recommendations that you make.

The level of detail required

Consider the following extract from a written observation of Jalah, aged three years and three months.

Aim: to observe and assess Jalah when she is mark-making.

Jalah picks up the red pencil with her left hand and, using a pincer grasp, transfers it to her right hand, she waves the pencil above her head and then moves it backwards and forwards across the paper. She puts the pencil down on the table and picks up a green one with her right hand. She repeats the backwards and forwards movements several times with the green pencil. She is trying to draw a rainbow.

Whilst this extract appears to be quite detailed it actually tells us nothing about Jalah's ability to use crayons or other mark-making materials. It does not record anything about her level of imagination or her ability to use language. The only thing that comes across clearly is that she is right-handed. Also, there is the assumption that Jalah is trying to draw a rainbow? This is a judgemental statement made by the observer. Now consider how much more conclusive the following observation would have been.

Aim: to observe and assess Jalah when she is mark-making.

Jalah is playing outside with a group of children. Her key worker asks her to come inside and draw a picture. Jalah nods, comes in and sits at the table. 'I don't know what to draw,' she says. 'Why don't you draw a rainbow, like the one we saw this morning?' says her key worker. Jalah nods and picks up a red pencil, she moves the pencil backwards and forwards over the paper. She then picks up another colour and repeats the action. 'I finished now' she says, 'Can I go outside?'

There is not a great deal of difference in the number of words used in each extract, but the second extract puts the activity into context – Jalah did not choose to do this activity, she was asked by her key worker, and although she complied, did not spend very long drawing the rainbow. We could assume that although Jalah was willing to draw, she was not really interested because she did not know what to draw, and would have possibly preferred to continue with her choice of activity. One conclusion that we could make which would affect future practice is that Jalah, or any other child for that matter, should not be removed from her chosen activity to draw without significant reason. In other words, as a form of assessment, with regard to the aim, this observation did not achieve its purpose.

It also highlights that the aim is too vague – why observe a child mark-making? What is the purpose? Is it to assess hand-eye coordination, fine motor skills, control, artistic ability, the understanding of instructions, or what precisely?

This is a good example of poor practice. Observations must have a clear purpose and should also be carried out at times during the day when the child is undertaking a range of activities. In conclusion, there is a clearly defined process for observations, which if followed, will determine the level of detail required. This process can be viewed in the flow chart shown below.

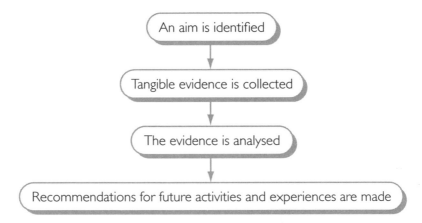

If this process is followed using any appropriate method or technique to record the evidence, then the practitioner will be in a very strong position to meet the child's individual needs and will therefore be able to plan appropriate activities and experiences.

Chapter 4 Linking observations to theoretical perspectives

How can evaluations be meaningful? How can realistic conclusions be drawn that will help the child or children progress?

There are numerous theorists and perspectives that can be considered and there will always be current research that either challenges or supports your views and theories. What is important is that observers look at current research as well as the knowledge of pioneers in the field. By doing this it is possible to increase your own understanding, improve your ability to evaluate and assess observations, and enable you to support children by providing appropriate activities and experiences which will meet their individual needs.

Considering the ideas and views of others through researching a topic, as well as using set texts, will in part answer the above questions. This will help develop an understanding of why children react and behave to certain situations and stimuli, and should help the observer make appropriate recommendations that meet the individual needs of the child.

Children react to stimuli in different ways

This chapter will consider:

◆ the value of theoretical perspectives

◆ evaluating different theories and perspectives

◆ how to make links between observed data and theories supported by examples.

Note that this chapter is not intended to be a detailed guide to theoretical perspectives. Its aim is to provide a starting point for further investigations and comparisons of theories in relation to observations. A chart of theorists and important researchers is provided at the end of the book for further reference (page 139).

The value of theoretical perspectives

How can theoretical perspectives develop knowledge and understanding? Why do practitioners need to consider theoretical perspectives?

Practitioners and students have been heard to say, 'well I know this information, why do I have to back it up with theorists, why can't you just take my word for it?'.

One of the main reasons for looking at theoretical perspectives is to enable the links between practice and theory to be made. Being able to make these links proves that the observer has a sound understanding of how children learn and develop. Linking theory with practice will enable practitioners to plan appropriate activities and experiences that will help the children develop and acquire new skills and knowledge.

What can be difficult is to know which theorists or perspectives to focus on initially, in other words, where to start. Some theorists appear to contradict each other or have opposing views. Jean Piaget and Sigmund Freud, for example, believed that development was stage-like, and that children progress through different stages as they mature. On the other hand, Lev Vygotsky and others saw the child as mainly influenced by culture and society. Theorists and researchers such as Albert Bandura put the view forward that development is not stage-like and focused on factors which lead to certain outcomes, such as the influences of adults, parents, carers, social and cultural influences, and the media.

THINK ABOUT IT

Bandura's social learning theory

Bandura's research showed that children learn through example. He found that a wide range of behaviours, such as sharing sex roles and aggressive actions, are learned as a result of children observing this behaviour in others. Social learning theory reinforces the need for children to see and model socially acceptable behaviours and positive role models. For example, if children hear adults using abusive language they will believe that this is an acceptable way to behave and will copy this behaviour; on the other hand if they see adults being altruistic, cooperative and caring then they will copy this behaviour.

It is now widely accepted that human development is a mix of both nature (genetic factors that we are born with) and nurture (environmental factors), and that humans undergo shifts in development.

THINK ABOUT IT

Nature versus nurture debate

This debate is about how much either nature (genetic inheritance/inborn abilities) or nurture (the environment – people, places and external influences) play a part in a child's development and learning.

If theorists believe nurture to be a strong influence, it means that the environment plays a more important role in a child's development than genetic traits. They believe that a child's early experiences will be the most important factor affecting their ability to achieve.

If theorists believe that nature is a strong influence it means that there is less importance on the environment because the potential to achieve is innate and children cannot perform at a higher level than their genetic influence will allow.

Relating theory to practice, if a child had learning difficulties then researchers following the nature approach could offer love and care, but might not expect the child to achieve very much at all, and would be unlikely to offer a stimulating environment because they believe that this would make little difference to the child's potential. Researchers following the nurture approach would believe that such a child should have a stimulating environment to make sure that they could achieve their full potential, whatever that may be.

It is important to note that apparently contrasting theories do not necessarily mean that one is right and the other is wrong. It is only through considering these theories and perspectives together with your own professional judgement about the needs of the child, that you will be able to decide upon the most appropriate course of action to enable them to progress.

Some students believe that there is little to be gained from looking at the ideas of academics who studied children in the past. But do we discount the process of evolution because Charles Darwin is a figure of the past?

THINK ABOUT IT

Piaget's theory of cognitive development

Piaget's belief that children develop schemas based on their direct experiences can help parents and practitioners understand why children's thinking is so different from adults. (Schemas are early ideas or concepts based on linked patterns of behaviour.) Piaget believed that from birth children actively select and interpret information from their environment. This is sometimes referred to as a constructivist approach because Piaget suggested that children build up or construct their thoughts according to their experiences of the world around them.

Piaget identified four broad stages of cognitive development:

1. Sensori-motor stage (0–2 years). Babies are reliant on their senses, especially touch and taste, and their first schemas are physical which lead to repetition of actions and control

2. Pre-operational stages (2–7 years). Children develop their skills at using language and symbols. They engage in much imaginative play where they use objects in a representational way, for example, cardboard boxes become cars. Piaget suggested that there were two further sub-stages within this one – pre-conceptual and intuitive – which have four main features running through them:
   - egocentrism – only being able to see things from their own perspective
   - conservation – children find it difficult to understand that things can remain the same even though the appearance may change
   - centration – children begin to classify objects and make associations
   - animism – children believe that objects have feelings, for example, the chair is naughty because it tripped me up.

3. Concrete operational stage (7–11 years). Children begin to use rules and strategies to help their thinking. They also use practical ways to solve problems such as using counters to find the answer to an addition sum

4. Formal operational stage (11–15 years). Children are now able to manipulate their ideas and thoughts to solve problems without using practical props.

Piaget's work has been very influential and widely accepted. However, recent work has shown that Piaget underestimated children's levels of thinking at different ages and that children could actually move through the stages more quickly if they are given experiences to help them.

Piaget's work and influence on early years provision has stimulated much research, an example being the Edinburgh group led by Margaret Donaldson in the 1970s. Piaget's ideas have provoked thought, discussion and research and will probably continue to do so for many years. In fact, much of today's research builds on Piaget's ideas, which are often used as a starting point for further work. The main critique of his work appears to be around the ages at which he felt children achieved certain skills. Even though his theory was developed in the past it still has value because it challenges what can be read, researched and observed.

Jean Piaget

The same argument can be applied to the work of John Bowlby, who developed the theory of attachment, which put forward the view that maternal attachment is essential for healthy psychological development. His theory was developed at a time when the majority of mothers did not work and there was little, if any, full day care provision for children. Following on from Bowlby, research by Emerson and Shaffer in 1964 concluded that babies and young children can develop multiple attachments, that is, attachments to more than one primary carer. In setting out his theory of attachment Bowlby's work led to a greater understanding of emotional development and, in particular, dependency and the need for emotional security. In a society where working career mothers are now commonplace, a greater understanding of the child's need to have consistent, caring relationships with adults will lead to better care for that child, with, for example, key workers in day nurseries and named nurses in paediatric wards. Key workers have become an accepted and very important role in many day nurseries and it can be argued that attachment theory supports this role. The Birth to Three Matters Framework (August 2002) places great importance on babies and young children developing relationships with close and protective adults.

THINK ABOUT IT

Bowlby's theory of attachment

Attachment theory, as originally defined by John Bowlby, states that babies need to form one main attachment (monotropy) that would be special and of more importance to the child than any other. Bowlby believed that children needed to develop this attachment by the end of their first year and that prolonged separation during the first four years from this special person would result in long-term psychological damage. He called this the 'critical period'. Bowlby showed through his research that meeting a child's physical and care needs is not enough for healthy development and growth. He suggested that children also needed consistent support which could be provided by the mother, although he changed his view on this in later years.

Bowlby also showed that children displayed distress when separated from their main attachment. He called this maternal deprivation and the distress is often referred to as separation anxiety. Bowlby believed that maternal deprivation in infancy could mean that children would not be able to form lasting relationships later in life.

Recent work has shown that children can develop multiple attachments, but in spite of this attachment theory is still very influential.

THINK ABOUT IT

Vygotsky's theory of cognitive development

Although Vygotsky's work was not published in the west until the early 1960s, he built on the theories of Piaget. Vygotsky thought that a child's social environment and experiences were very important. He believed that children were social beings from birth and that through interactions with their parents, and later peers, they acquired skills and concepts. He suggested that adults needed to extend children's learning to enable them to reach their full potential, and called this the zone of proximal development (ZPD). His belief was that adults need to intervene in order to help children move into the ZPD. Like Piaget, Vygotsky saw children as active learners, but believed social interactions were needed for intellectual growth and development.

Vygotsky suggested that thought and language begin as two separate activities, for example, when a baby babbles and coos they are not using these sounds as a way of thinking. He also suggested that at around two years old language and thought development merge and children begin to use language to express their thoughts and ideas.

Pioneer theorists such as Piaget and Vygotsky provided the building blocks on which to develop and extend our ideas and, in doing so, increase our own understanding and knowledge of children's development. This will inevitably lead to us planning and developing more appropriate and better provision for the children.

How to make links between observed data and theories

As discussed earlier some theories appear to adopt different perspectives and interpretations of development. This can make it confusing when considering which perspective to reflect on. It is important that practitioners do not try to look for perspectives that conveniently 'fit' what they have observed. It is good practice to look for information about a topic that will include different perspectives. As a possible suggested starting point to help you look at perspectives consider again the aim of an observation. Ask yourself:

◆ What was I trying to find out?

◆ Why?

It could be argued that all of the theories mentioned above are relevant, however, as the objective was to assess interaction perhaps Vygotsky's theory is the most appropriate for the observer to consider. The recommendations could be that the setting needs to consider the role of adults in supporting children's play and in so doing, stimulate the learning and language development of the children. On the other hand, it would be perfectly reasonable to focus on play opportunities and provision, which could also lead to consideration of the role of the adult and the planning within the setting. Note that you may have come to a different but equally valid conclusion.

So how do you decide which theorist or perspective is the most suitable and relevant for your observation? The following five steps should help.

Step 1

Look again at your **aim** and if necessary underline it or use a highlighter pen, but make sure you are really focused on what you have observed.

Step 2

Look again at your **objective** and do the same as you did for the aim.

THINK ABOUT IT

A student has made a written observation of two boys playing together with small-scale toys. Their ages are two years nine months and two years two months. The aim of the observation was to observe the children's language development and the objective was to assess their level of verbal interaction. The observation evidence shows that the boys did not talk very much during their play, they did not play with the toys, and spent much of the time watching another group of children playing on a climbing frame.

This evidence could be interpreted in several different ways.

◆ The observer could conclude that these boys had not yet reached Piaget's stage of pre-operational development, as they did not use the toys as symbols in their play. (Symbolism is a key feature of this stage of Piaget's theory.) In addition they did not use language to develop their play.

◆ On the other hand, this observation evidence could relate to Vygotsky's theory on the social context of learning. An adult playing alongside the boys may have extended the play and moved the boys into the 'zone of proximal development'.

◆ What about the level of play and the apparent lack of motivation? This could lead to research on Abraham Maslow's theories of motivation.

◆ Had the boys been told to play together? Were the toys of their choosing? This could lead to consideration of Susan Isaacs and her views on play, and also the researcher Janet Moyles.

The practitioner would also need to think about:

◆ language development and play development including pretend play, even though this was not part of the aim, but could have been evident in the observation

◆ emotional and social development.

So which is relevant to this observation?

Step 3

Go through the evidence of your observation very carefully and underline or highlight all the evidence that relates **directly** to the aim and objective. (If whilst doing this you discover that you actually have very little evidence to support your aim and objective, it may be necessary to do another observation.) Also, make a note of what else you may have learned and what information may be useful to extend your understanding of this child or children.

Step 4

Look in textbooks, professional journals, websites and any other places you think are appropriate for views, perspectives and theories which relate directly to your aim and objective.

Step 5

Look at the evidence that you have underlined and reflect on what your research has taught you.

Below is a typed example of a written observation where the observer has followed the steps outlined above.

Step 1

Aim: to look at the **emotional development** of a child aged three years old.

Step 2

Objective: to comment on and assess how this child responds to **being separated from her mother** in order to find ways of supporting the child and helping the parent. (Note that the mother is often running late and this distress for S is not unusual, hence the reason for the observation.)

Step 3

Observation evidence – description

Child S is carried into the nursery by her mother. She has both arms around her mother's neck and is burying her face in mum's neck. The adult approaches and greets both the child and the parent. Mum responds, but S does not. Mum bends down and starts to take S's jacket off telling the adult that she is in a hurry this morning as they are 'running' late. The adult takes S's jacket and hangs it up then holds out her hand to S. Mum pulls S's arms off her neck and tells her that she has to go. She gives S a quick kiss and moves towards the door. S starts to cry and makes to follow mum. The adult bends down and takes hold of S's hand, mum waves goodbye and the adult urges S to do the same, but she does not respond. The adult starts to talk quietly to S and wipes her face with a tissue. S is still crying quietly and is sucking her right thumb. S and the adult move in the main room and go and sit on the carpet with the other children.

Step 4

Looked in the following for ideas on recommending strategies on how to make separation from parents less stressful and ideas on understanding the child's behaviour:

Tassoni P. et al, 2002. *Diploma in Childcare and Education*. Oxford, Heinemann

Davenport, 1993. *An introduction to Child Development*. Collins

Riddall-Leech, S. 2003. *Managing Children's Behaviour*. Oxford, Heinemann

www.parentlineplus.org

Birth to Three Framework Literature Review (2002)

Step 5

Considered Bowlby's theory of attachment and the work and research of the Robertsons (1950–60), Ainsworth (1978), Schaffer and Emerson (1964), Goldschmeid and Selleck (1996), Clark and Clark (2000) and Braungart-Reiker et al (2001). Decided to focus on separation anxiety and will make recommendations of how to minimise the adverse effects for S. Need to find out more about the role of the key worker/person in day care settings.

NOTE TO STUDENTS

Separation anxiety can also refer to the shift in development which occurs around eight months when babies become wary of strangers. In this example it might be helpful for consideration to be given for the reasons for the distress, the behaviour of the mother and how to support both her and the child.

Evaluating different theories and perspectives

First of all let us consider what is meant by 'evaluating' or 'evaluation'. If you evaluate something you consider its strengths and weaknesses. Observations must be evaluated and/or assessed in order to come to some conclusions about the child and support the thinking about what to do next. It is important to note that the primary focus of a practitioner is not to evaluate or critically analyse a theoretical perspective, but this can be a requirement for students to gain higher grades. Practitioners need to find information which supports their understanding and consider whether or not it 'sheds light' on their problem.

TRY IT OUT

Now try to evaluate a different theoretical perspective such as Vygotsky's theory of the social context of learning, Susan Isaacs' views on the importance of play, or Lawrence Kohlberg's views on moral development. If it is helpful make a table like the one evaluating aspects of Piaget's theory. Try to link some of the strengths and weaknesses to observations that have been have carried out.

As a starting point some students may find it helpful to evaluate a theory or theoretical perspective by making lists, or charts with columns, as shown below.

An evaluation of Piaget's theory of cognitive development	
Strengths	Weaknesses
Piaget was trying to find the main stages of cognitive development, and at what ages these stages might occur.	Not all researchers believe development is stage-like, for instance the behaviourists believe that development is continuous.
Piaget took a 'clinical' approach to his tests, asking children very specific questions.	The clinical approach can be rather vague and open to interpretation by the person asking the questions. There is also the danger of 'leading' the child to give certain answers.
Piaget suggested that logical thought develops around puberty.	More recent research has shown that adolescents and many adults are not always capable of logical thought, but this does not mean that in 'normal' development, this transition is not achievable.
Piaget developed key terms such as 'equilibrium' to try to show how thinking is organised.	Some of Piaget's terms are criticised for being too general (Margaret Donaldson, 1978).
Piaget claimed that he was aware of individual differences.	Piaget was always looking for what the 'average' child could do and so ignored the great individual variations on how children think, or the factors that may affect their thinking.
Piaget was a pioneer in developing a theory of cognitive development.	Modern researchers, such as Martin Hughes, McGarrigle and Donaldson, criticise Piaget's work as being too complicated, but although the theory has been widely challenged, it has stimulated a huge amount of further research.

The table above is by no means complete but it is a start. However, you may not need all of the points listed above to evaluate a theory or a perspective, two or three would suffice in some cases. You should try to pick out the points to evaluate that you can relate back to the children or child in your observation and evidence.

How theoretical knowledge can support and develop practice

Adults who live and work with babies and young children will acquire an abundance of anecdotal evidence. However, such evidence can be unreliable and subjective. For instance, many parents believe that their child can do things that they are not actually capable of, often not because they want their child to be better, faster or cleverer than others, but because they are emotionally involved with their child, and emotions can cloud judgement. Also, some parents may not want to admit that there might be a cause for concern with their child, they may feel guilty and blame themselves.

A future architect?

CASE STUDY

Jan and her partner both work full-time and have placed their seven month old baby with a childminder. The childminder has become aware that the baby does not appear to respond to sounds, especially those out of his line of vision such as the telephone, although he is beginning to babble. The childminder talks to the parents about her concerns, but Jan insists that there is no problem when the baby is at home and suggests that the childminder's house is too noisy for her baby to distinguish particular sounds. However, the childminder is not convinced that this is the case. She does a series of observations during quiet times of the day and discovers that the baby will respond when he has full eye contact or when he can see the object that is making the noise. He does not respond to sounds that are out of his line of vision. The childminder again talks to the parents and shows them her observations and explains how she has reached her conclusion. She suggests that the parents do similar observations at home and then compare their findings. Jan does this and has to admit that her baby does not appear to be able to hear things that are out of his line of vision. A follow-up visit to the GP shows that the baby has limited hearing in one ear.

In the above case study the childminder had knowledge of child development and developmental milestones. They also knew that in the pre-linguistic stage of language development a baby of this age could be expected to respond to sounds. Also, she was aware that language and communication skills can be learned through reinforcement (B. F. Skinner) and if the baby did not respond then reinforcement could not take place. This is an example of how knowledge of theoretical perspectives can improve, support and develop professional practice. However, whilst language is learned by reinforcement in one sense, in that the baby responds to sounds, this type of reinforcement does not strictly relate to the behaviourist's meaning of the word. This is one of the main criticisms of the behaviourist approach to language development as it does not explain spontaneous speech or the idiosyncratic speech that older children use. So, while the childminder has supported the child's development and met their needs, this is an example of where further research and reading would have been helpful because Skinner's perspective is only one approach to language development.

B.F. Skinner

THINK ABOUT IT

Skinner's theory of reinforcement

Skinner's theory of reinforcement is a 'nurture' theory because he suggests that children learn if their efforts are reinforced in some way. For example, a baby smiles or gurgles, then the parent or main carer smiles and says something positive in pleasing tones so the baby gets emotional satisfaction and learns to smile or gurgle again to get the same response from the adult. Skinner used this idea to suggest that babies and young children stop making some sounds if adults did not recognise or respond to the sounds. Because the adult did not reinforce the action the baby would not repeat it. Skinner called this process selective reinforcement.

Linking theories, theoretical perspectives, practical work and professional practice shows understanding of the theory or perspective involved.

Below is another example of how an observer has linked theory to practice. (This is only a section of the observation.) The observer has considered two theoretical perspectives and has used these views to make practical suggestions of how to develop the professional practice of the adults in the setting and stimulate the development of the child.

Aim: to look at incidences of difficult or challenging behaviour in a boy aged four years and three months.

Objective: to consider reasons for the behaviour and to plan appropriate activities to manage this behaviour effectively.

Method: event sample.

Background information: K's parents have recently split up following a violent relationship over the last two years.

Name of observer:

Date of observation:

Name of child: Kyle

Age: 4 years and 3 months

Event	Date and time	Situation	Comment
1	07.07.04 9.20a.m.	K is on the carpet during circle time	K is poking the child next to him, the adult asks him to stop He stops poking the girl, then hits her on the arm. Child cries, K is moved to sit with another adult
2	07.07.04 10.10a.m.	K is playing with cars and a garage in a group of three children	K wants a car that another child has. K hits the girl twice, girl starts to cry, K is moved away by an adult
3	07.07.04 10.30a.m.	K is washing his hands	K is jumping around the toilet area, he bumps into several children. An adult asks him to stop
4	07.07.04 10.3 a.m.	At the snack area	K pushes in front of a girl to get a piece of fruit
5	07.07.04 11.05a.m.	In the garden	K and a girl start to fight over a trike, K starts to hit the girl. The adult moves K away
6	07.07.04 11.30a.m.	Story time	K pushes another child over and shouts that he can't see the pictures
7	09.07.04 9.45a.m.	At the craft table	K has a pair of scissors, he threatens to 'cut D's nose off'. D (female) has a card tube that K wants. The adult takes the scissors away from K, who starts to cry
8	09.07.04 10.45a.m.	In the garden	K is kicking a football, he then kicks a girl. The adult moves K away
9	09.07.04 11.10a.m.	At the computer	K and S are playing together, they start to fight over who will move the mouse. The adult moves both boys away

Conclusions

K exhibits difficult and challenging behaviours during the session, especially when he is in group situations. It would seem that when he can't get what he wants he hits out or pushes other children out of his way. This causes distress to the other children and each time an adult intervenes. The observation shows that the incidences of aggression are often directed towards girls. In discussions with K's mum we know that her partner has been violent towards her, and that these events have been witnessed by K. The social learning theory developed by Albert Bandura suggests that children can learn aggressive acts from role models. The setting does not allow violent or aggressive behaviour under any circumstances so we can draw the conclusion that K has learned this behaviour elsewhere. However, social learning theory cannot explain why K is aggressive when playing, his possible role model would not have been in this situation, so how could he have learned to react in this way? A colleague suggests that it is his aggression to girls that is important, given his background.

Overall we feel that K needs to learn from other role models who do not exhibit aggressive behaviour towards anyone.

The observation also shows that he gets attention from adults when he is aggressive. A colleague has suggested that this is reinforcing the behaviour, so he gets aggressive when he wants attention. This is supported by B.F. Skinner who suggested that if an action is reinforced in a positive way a child will repeat the action. In K's case the positive reinforcement is our attention.

What we are going to do:

- share our observation and conclusions with K's mum. We will also ask her how he is with her at home and with other family members and adults

- make sure that we all give K attention, praise, eye contact, and verbal comments when he is calm, playing and interacting well. We will tell him that we enjoy playing with him and watching him play with other children

- when he is acting inappropriately we will move him away, but will give him minimal eye contact, or avoid talking to him much, in other words we will keep our interactions low key

- we will try to be positive role models for K, and will also try to make sure he sees us interacting in a positive, warm and caring way with all children and all parents

- we will have a consistent approach by all the adults to all of the children

- we will review this action plan in one month and discuss with K's mum and staff any changes.

THINK ABOUT IT

It is true that children can learn aggressive behaviour as set out in Bandura's social learning theory, but this is far from the whole story. The child in the observation example above has an emotional reaction to events and, while his father was violent, it is not clear what the relationship was between the child and his father, as well as his mother. There is work by Bruce Perry (1994) about the impact of violence on children which would be useful in this case. There is also a potential issue with the boy's aggression towards girls, but this is not exclusive. This child is angry, hurt and confused so it would be useful for practitioners to think about issues around attachment and trauma. They could also find out about positive behaviour strategies.

At the end of this book there is a chart of theorists and important researchers who have developed the work of others. This chart is by no means complete, but should be regarded as a starting point for further investigations and research.

Chapter 5 Linking observations to developmental norms

Linking observations to developmental norms is an effective way of linking theory to practice. Developmental norms are often presented in areas of development such as physical, cognitive/intellectual, social, emotional and language. So by definition they cannot be holistic in themselves. However, this does not devalue the use of developmental norms to assess and measure development.

Most early years professionals divide a child's development into different areas so that the child's progress and growth can be measured and assessed. However, we must remember that all areas of development are inter-related, so the environment in which a child is brought up and the people with whom they interact will have a powerful influence on their development. All development areas are linked in some way, for example, language development can affect social development, and in the same way an activity planned to promote specific physical skills can also help develop language and social skills.

One way to look at how a child develops is to divide life into stages. Piaget and Freud believed that development was stage-like. Children develop as they grow and although the speed at which they develop varies, it is suggested that all children pass through the same stages of development, but not at the same rate. Each stage of development is clearly defined, for example, a baby sits up before crawling, and stands before walking. These are norms

Walking is the end result of several developmental stages

or milestones of development. A child must pass through one stage of development before they can move on to the next stage.

Some theorists view development in a different way, believing that it is an unbroken progression, and that stages are hard to separate. This idea focuses on factors that lead to certain outcomes, such as the influence of parents, family members, peers, and the media on the development of gender, self, moral attitudes, behaviour, aggression, emotion and play. For example, Erik Erikson accepted Freud's idea that development is stage-like, but believed that parents have a very important influence on their child's development. Whether we agree that development is stage-like or continuous we will find that we use some form of measurement or norm to assess development and progression.

This chapter will consider:

◆ the value of developmental norms

◆ using observations to plan age, stage appropriate activities and support practice

◆ percentile charts.

The value of developmental norms

Almost as far back as written records go we can find evidence that shows how excited human beings become over growth and development. We have a fascination with measuring and evaluating growth by comparing and drawing parallels with others. In the eighteenth century western European scientists used seasonal and day and night metaphors as yardsticks for growth and development. The table below lists a few of these measurement systems.

Chronological age (in years)	Time of year	Time of day
Birth–2	Frozen	Before daybreak
2–7	Thawing	Dawn
7–14	Budding	Daybreak
14–21	Leafing out	Sunrise
21–28	Blossoming	Breakfast
28–35	Increasing in size	Before noon
35–42	Maturing	Noon
42–49	Reaping	Afternoon
49–56	Spreading about	Dinner
56–63	Falling of leaves	Sunset
65–70	Freezing	Twilight
70–death	Winter time	Night

Adapted from Wadstroem, 1769 in Daehler B, 1992.

Perhaps this is where we get the expressions 'middle-age-spread' and the 'twilight years'?

Today we have more precise ways of determining norms. The measurement and assessment of children's development is based on studies of children of all ages going back for many years. Mary Sheridan's valuable research in the 1950s provided a framework for assessing and measuring development, and these measurements became known as developmental norms or milestones.

What are developmental norms?

Norms are quantitative measurements that provide typical values and variations in height, weight, language and so on. These norms have become an essential yardstick for attempting to answer questions about how biological and environmental factors can affect development. We now know that a baby may begin to smile at around 6 weeks, that most children can walk steadily while carrying something at 18 months, that most 3 year olds make friends and are interested in having friends, and that most 5 year olds show an interest in reading and writing. These are called developmental norms or milestones.

Developmental norms are valued because they satisfy the curiosity of adults about what a child should be doing at a given age. Having this type of knowledge also helps adults to predict what might happen next in a child's development. This makes us feel secure and ultimately helps us to be more confident and effective in caring for children and planning appropriate activities.

Developmental norms give us background information and a framework within which we can assess developmental progress or delay through observing children. Having information with which to compare or assess development can help us provide developmentally appropriate activities for a child that will meet their individual needs and enable them to progress.

There will be occasions in which we will need to assess a child's progress after illness or an accident. Using developmental norms to measure progress can help us decide if the child needs additional help or support. After measuring progress we can plan appropriate activities for the child that aid their development.

At the end of the book there is a chart of developmental norms and theorists associated with them. This chart is by no means complete, but can be regarded as a starting point for further investigations and research.

As human beings, we must achieve one developmental norm before we can strive to meet the next. For example, we must be able to crawl before we can walk and we must be competent walkers before we can run, and so on. If all children mature at approximately the same age and we all pass the same stages of development, why aren't all children the same?

The answer lies in our genes and in our emotional, social and cultural environment. Each person has a unique genetic structure; some people have genes that contribute to the development of very early motor skills, and can move around at an early stage in their development, whilst others cannot. Genes can influence certain aspects of developmental maturation, cognitive potential and physical skills. In part, they explain why some babies can stand at six months and others cannot stand until 11 months. Both babies may still be within developmental norms, which usually record babies as moving around in some way by the age of nine months.

It is important to note that genes do not explain the variety of individual human perspectives, responses, behaviours and motivations. Developmental norms are averages that have been recorded over many years, meaning that there will always be some individuals who are quicker or slower to reach them.

Whilst it is important that we recognise the value of using developmental norms to measure and assess development, it is also very important that we recognise the disadvantages of using developmental norms. Some adults may become concerned if they think a child is below a developmental norm, and may label that child as 'developmentally delayed', conversely labelling the child as 'advanced' if they are above the developmental norm. There is also the danger of thinking that a child is impaired in some area when they may simply be slower to develop in one way than in others.

We must learn to crawl before we can move on to walking

Look at the following checklist observation extract completed by a childcare student on a Level 3 course.

Aim: to compare the fine motor skills of three five year olds.

Objective: to compare and assess fine motor skill development using developmental norms.

Setting: reception class – children were observed over the course of one day as they were engaged in various activities.

Skill	Child A (Male) 5 years 2 months	Child B (Female) 5 years 3 months	Child C (Male) 5 years 6 months
Can use a knife and fork	Can use fork, needs help with knife	Yes	Yes
Can thread a large eyed needle	Yes	Yes	Yes
Uses a dynamic tripod grasp to hold a pencil	No	Yes	No
Can form the letters of their own name	No	Yes	Only the first 3 (name has 6 letters)
Can draw a person with a body, head, legs, nose, mouth and eyes	Yes	Yes	Yes
Can draw around a template	Yes	Yes	Yes
Can count the fingers of one hand using the index finger of the other	No	No	Yes
Can complete a 20 piece jigsaw puzzle with interlocking pieces	No	Yes	No
Can cut out shapes using scissors	Yes	Yes	Yes
Can fasten a button into a buttonhole	No	Yes	No

Checklist skills taken from Meggit and Sunderland (2002) and Tassoni et al (2002).

This student has clearly used recognised textbooks to develop the checklist of skills, and these relate to the developmental norms/milestones for five year olds. The observation clearly shows that the three children are developing at different rates because they are not all meeting every one of the chosen developmental norms. This reinforces the idea that every child is unique.

At first glance this observation could be interpreted in a way which could imply that child A is developmentally delayed because he cannot meet six out of ten norms. This is perhaps a situation that could cause unnecessary anxiety and concern for a parent or carer as this child does not appear to be achieving the milestones considered normal in a five year old. On the other hand, this is the youngest child and he *can* meet 4 of the norms for five year olds.

This form of checklist observation does not provide any evidence or data on the general state of health of the children or any other factors that could affect the children's performance, for example, anxiety levels, disinterest in the activity, and social skills. Normative assessment presented in this way has drawbacks and people should be encouraged to use other observation techniques before drawing any firm conclusions about lack of progress.

Consider this extract from a written observation.

Aim: to observe the language development of a two and half year old girl.

Objective: to assess vocabulary development.

Age of child: 2 years and 4 months   Gender: Female (known as B)

Setting: the quiet area of a pre-school playgroup in a community hall. The area is separated from the rest of the hall by low shelf units and furnished with large cushions and a rug.

B and the adult are sat together looking at B's favourite storybook – The Very Hungry Caterpillar. The adult points to the first page, 'What's this B?' she asks, 'Leaf,' B replies and turns the page.

'Look, pillar' says B.

'Yes it's the caterpillar,' says the adult, 'and there's the sun.'

'Sun' says B and turns the page.

'What's this?' asks the adult.

'Apple' says B pointing to the picture, 'pillar apple'.

'Yes, the caterpillar eats the apple' says the adult, 'he eats 2 pears as well.'

'Pears well' says B.

'Let's count the plums' says the adult pointing to the pictures, 'one, two, three.'

'two, three' repeats B.

From this extract it can be seen that B repeats words that are said to her, this is known as echolalia. She uses two word phrases to express meaning such as 'pillar apple' which could mean that the caterpillar eats the apple. This is often referred to as telegraphic speech or telegraphese. From these two examples it would be possible to look at the developmental milestones/norms for language development of two year olds and assess if B is meeting them.

In this case the developmental norms show that this girl is progressing as would be expected for a child of her age. There is no attempt to compare her development with another child. Armed with the information that the child is progressing the adult can plan activities and experiences that will stimulate their development.

TRY IT OUT

Plan to do a series of observations on individual children of different ages. Try to do different aspects of development for each observation.

For example:
Physical development of a baby under a year.
Social development of a child between one and two years old.
Emotional development of a three year old.
Language development of a four year old.
Cognitive development of a five year old.
Physical development of a six year old.
Social development of a seven year old.

These examples could be part of your aim.

Use developmental milestones/norms to assess the progress of the child, this would be part of your objective.

Doing a series of observations in this way will help you to become more familiar with the developmental norms.

To help B move on the adult could plan activities that provide opportunities for them to ask questions and name objects and pictures. They could also use finger puppets and props to retell the story, or B could represent the story through her own drawings and be encouraged to talk about, name and count the objects mentioned within the story.

Percentile charts

Percentile charts use developmental norms to assess and measure development, and are often used by health visitors and other medical professionals to measure the development of babies. They are specially prepared charts used to record measurements of growth. Each chart is based on thousands of measurements taken of babies at different ages over many years, which are then averaged out. From this data a graph can be drawn to show a measure of development, and an individual baby's measurements can then be taken and recorded against the percentile chart. There are different percentile charts to measure weight, height, head circumference and other physical skills.

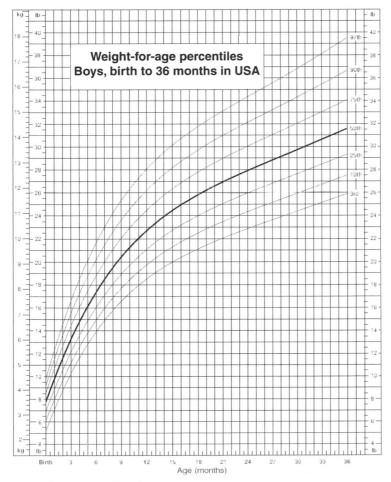

Example percentile chart

Percentile charts are used to measure and record an individual child's progress and healthcare professionals will only compare the child to the norms, or percentiles, shown on the chart. Some charts are printed with the 3rd and 10th percentiles, the 3rd percentile being the bottom line on the chart. As a rough guide, if a child's measurements fall below the 3rd percentile healthcare professionals will have concerns because they may be failing, so action should be taken to help them.

THINK ABOUT IT

Read the following short pieces of information then try to decide if these children are showing learning and behaviour that is characteristic for their age, in other words learning and behaviour which matches to the appropriate developmental norm.

An eighteen month old crawling downstairs unaided.
A five year old competently using a knife and fork.
A four year old matches three primary colours.
A two year old with a vocabulary of over two hundred words.
A six year old with a clear sense of right and wrong.
A six month old baby reaching for and grabbing a toy with both hands.

Using observations to plan and stage appropriate activities

Observations and the planning of activities are inextricably linked. Effective planning should be in the form of a continuous cycle, such as that shown in the simple diagram below.

Plan

Activities that are planned should take into account a child's age, stage of development and their individual needs. The stage of development and individual needs can only be effectively assessed through some form of observation. When we observe and assess the developmental stage of the child we should become aware of their needs. In doing so, any activities that we plan are more likely to be appropriate and should develop and expand the child's knowledge and skill acquisition.

It is also important that activities planned take into account a child's interests, this information can also be acquired through observing the child, talking and listening to them and then recording your findings. Children are more likely to play, learn and develop if the activities in which they are involved interest and stimulate them.

The form that your planning takes can be varied. Some professionals follow proforma sheets to help them plan activities, but some actually write down very little. The format of planning is to a certain extent irrelevant, what is important is that the planning uses the evidence of observations to provide stimulating and appropriate activities.

CASE STUDIES

1. Ameera noticed that Jaleh, aged seven months, was trying to roll over from her back to her stomach, but not quite making it. Ameera thought (her planning) that if she placed interesting toys and objects just out of Jaleh's reach, she would be encouraged to roll over.

2. Paul observed that Tom and Daisy, twins aged two years and five months, would sit on their tricycles and propel them along with their feet, but they would not use the pedals. He decided to encourage the children to play on a wider range of ride-on toys to support the development of their coordination skills.

3. Wesley's classroom assistant had observed that he did not find writing down his ideas, feelings and thoughts an easy task. She knew that Wesley enjoyed playing in the puppet theatre and thought that it might help Wesley if he could use puppets to express himself (Wesley is six years and eleven months old).

In each of the case studies above the childcare practitioner observed the child in some shape or form and used the evidence of the observations to plan appropriate activities or experiences. However, were the expectations of the practitioners appropriate?

Implement

To implement something means to put it into practice, so you would take the evidence of your observations, plan a suitable activity and then carry it out. As the plans have been informed by the evidence of observations it should follow that the planned activities and experiences meet the needs of the children.

However, sometimes we get things wrong. We might have observed a child, but arrived at an incorrect or inappropriate conclusion. If so, the activity that we plan and implement will not meet the needs of the child satisfactorily. This supports the argument that we should observe a child on more than one occasion before making firm conclusions.

CASE STUDIES

1. When Jaleh was on the carpet, Ameera placed several attractive and interesting objects just out of her reach. This encouraged Jaleh to move in order to reach the items.

2. When the children were outside Paul joined in the play that involved ride-on toys and push-and-pull toys travelling along a 'road' track. He hoped this would support the children in their play and aid the development of their skills.

3. After circle time Wesley and the classroom assistant took some puppets to his table. Wesley made up a story about shopping at the supermarket using the puppets. He pretended that one of the puppets got cross because the 'mum' puppet wouldn't buy some crisps.

The implementation of these planned activities is not the end of the process as far as observing children is concerned. How do we know that the needs of the children were met, or that they had opportunities to extend and develop their skills? These questions lead us into the next part of the process.

Review

When we review something we take another look at it, re-examining the situation or activity. We need to ask ourselves some questions, such as:

◆ Did this activity or experience achieve what I had hoped? In other words, did I meet my aim?

◆ Did the child or children react and respond in the way that I had expected?

◆ Was it an appropriate activity or experience for this child at this time? In other words, did it meet their needs?

◆ Did I have enough resources or equipment for this activity or experience?

◆ Did I have enough time to get everything ready before the activity or experience? And was there enough time during and afterwards to tidy up or clear away?

CASE STUDIES

1. Ameera noted that Jaleh made several attempts to reach the objects before she finally rolled over. Jaleh was contentedly occupied for ten minutes, however, one or two of the items were too close to the baby and actually hindered her movements. Ameera made brief written comments about what Jaleh did in a notebook.

2. Tom and Daisy stayed in the play situation with Paul for a very short time, then they both went over to the climbing frame. Paul made a mental note to write this information on the children's record sheets.

3. Wesley asked the classroom assistant to write down his story for him so that he could draw a picture of the puppets in the supermarket. They ran out of time because they had to go the hall for P.E.

Evaluate

An evaluation looks at the strengths and weaknesses of a situation, and by using these we can we assess the value of the activity or experience. To do this effectively we need evidence, data, or firm facts, which acts as the evidence of observations. In all three case studies the childcare practitioner had evidence to support their evaluation of the planned activity or experience. Ameera had written notes, Paul relied on his memory to write down information in the children's records and the classroom assistant had the unfinished story and drawing to support her evaluation. As a result of this evidence all three individuals will be able to plan more activities and experiences to support the children in their care.

1. Ameera came to the conclusion that Jaleh would benefit from this experience again as she took several attempts to roll over. Ameera also decided that she needed fewer items and to put them further way from Jaleh.

2. Paul was disappointed that Tom and Daisy stayed in the play situation with him for such a short time. He felt that his presence had actually hindered the play rather than stimulating it. He decided that he would observe the children again when playing outside and plan opportunities to develop their coordination skills through kicking, throwing and catching large balls.

3. Wesley's classroom assistant felt that Wesley had responded in a positive way to the activity and expressed disappointment when they had to stop before it was finished. She decided to try the activity again but this time write down the story as Wesley acted it out, and so give him time to draw a picture.

In each of these case studies the practitioners have used observations to support their practice. They have observed throughout the planning process and so will have been able to meet the needs of the children more effectively.

In practical terms you may not think that you would be able to observe at each and every stage of the planning process. Practitioners are very busy and may not have the luxury of time to 'stand back' and observe. However, the amount that is actually recorded will vary from situation to situation and will also depend on which point each person is at in the planning process. There may not be the opportunity to write down the results of observations immediately after the activity, although it is good practice to try to do so. It may be necessary to rely on memory or the comments of other colleagues. However, the most important aspect is that recognition is given to the value and importance of using observational evidence to support planning, and so strengthen and develop professional practice.

Chapter 6 Linking observations to the Birth to Three Matters Framework

The Birth to Three Matters Framework is designed to support all those who work with young children from birth to three years. It focuses primarily on the child, not on subjects or areas of development. The framework places great importance on observing children and using this information to plan appropriate activities and experiences for them.

The Birth to Three Matters Framework identifies four aspects:

◆ a strong child

◆ a skilful communicator

◆ a competent learner

◆ a healthy child.

Each aspect is divided into four components. Among the materials included in the Birth to Three Matters pack are colour-coded cards for each component, 16 in

> **Look, listen, note**
> • Observe and note the sounds and facial expressions young babies make in response to affectionate attention from their parent or their key person.
> • Note verbal and non-verbal expressions of feelings which take place when babies are changed, fed, cuddled etc.
> • Observe sounds and facial expressions as young children express feelings of frustration, anger or as they separate from a carer.
> • Note examples of healthy independence; e.g. a child playing happily with building blocks, or looking through a window.

Example of part of a colour-coded card from The Birth to Three Matters Framework

total. An important section on all of these cards, as far as this book is concerned, is the part entitled 'Look, listen, note'.

There is also a CD-ROM in the Birth to Three Matters pack with a wealth of information on it to help practitioners understand how the framework can support their practice. Reference is made throughout this chapter to this CD-ROM, suggesting that the reader accesses the information to research and read around a topic in order to extend and develop their understanding and knowledge. However, this does not mean that the Birth to Three Matters CD-ROM should be used exclusively, because it is good practice to consider as many different sources of information as possible when researching a particular topic or aspect of development.

This chapter will look at each of the Birth to Three Matters Framework aspects in turn, using case studies and examples of observations to consider how the framework can support, inform, challenge and guide people working with young children from birth to three years old. It will also look at how the aspects assist in the observation and planning process.

A strong child

Refer to the purple cards in the Birth to Three Matters pack.

While the aspect of 'A strong child' can stand alone, in reality it runs throughout the entire framework. The term 'a strong child' does not refer to a physically strong child, but to an emotionally strong child; one who is confident, capable and self-assured. An important factor in the development of a strong child is living within a nurturing environment in which they can become aware of their own capabilities, gain confidence, develop self-assurance and be able to explore the world in which they live from a safe and stable base. In order to do all of these things children need a caring and sensitive adult who can support their development, as well as plan and provide appropriate opportunities for growth. The adult must be able to meet their needs and one way to do this effectively is to undertake regular observations. The framework refers to this individual as the 'key person'.

Babies are very interested in other people from birth, and during the first few months of life they try to form close relationships with significant people, usually a parent or close relative. They are also able to form relationships with other people, such as early years practitioners or a key person. The framework describes the key person or people as those individuals who know the child well, and who are able to respond to their gestures and cues. They provide familiarity, pattern, and predictability, all of which gives older babies a sense of being themselves.

THINK ABOUT IT

In recent years there has been much research on the importance of children forming secure attachments with caring adults. John Bowlby was one of the first people to consider and acknowledge the need to form attachments, having observed children in orphanages and other such institutions. He concluded that children deprived of a secure relationship with one caring adult in their very early years, especially their mother, were more likely to have behavioural concerns as they grew up. However, more recent research has challenged and developed Bowlby's work so we now recognise that babies can make secure attachments to several people (Forrest, 1997). Bowlby's work has prompted a wealth of research on issues about attachment. For example, Mary Ainsworth (1967) studied babies in America and Africa and how they made attachments. She argued that the measure of the attachment was the baby's response when their mother returned to them after an interval of absence. Elfer et al (2002) considered the practical difficulties that staff in group care settings encounter when attempting to achieve close relationships with young children. They looked at many issues including the impact of staff rotas and shift patterns, holidays, staff changes due to promotion, and how children of different ages can be provided with new and varied experiences. More information on this topic can be found on the Birth to Three Matters CD-ROM.

A key person:

◆ helps a baby and young child cope throughout the day

◆ frequently observes and assesses the baby and/or young child in order to meet their individual needs

◆ thinks about the child and may worry about them

◆ knows them very well, understands and appreciates their likes, dislikes and personal preferences

◆ talks to the baby and/or child and talks about them with their colleagues.

While the key person is crucial to the aspect of a strong child, this special

A key person is crucial to the aspect of a strong child

relationship is equally important to the other three aspects within the Birth to Three Matters Framework. All of the aspects are inter-related and all contribute to enabling the child to reach their full potential.

The four components of 'A strong child' are:

◆ me, myself and I

◆ being acknowledged and affirmed

◆ developing self assurance

◆ a sense of belonging.

Me, myself and I

This component considers how babies and young children become aware of themselves as individuals and how they learn that they can influence others as well as being influenced. It looks at how children begin to understand similarities and differences, and show preferences and specific interests in their play and experiences.

CASE STUDY

Jess is a nanny working with a private family during the day. She cares for Angus, who is three months old. Jess observed that Angus had started to move his head and eyes towards the sound of her voice when she went to him after his nap. From this observation Jess placed a mobile above his cot. She noticed that after a few days Angus moved his head and eyes to follow the movements of the mobile, and also waved his arms in the direction of the mobile.

This is an example of the component 'Me, myself and I'. Angus was beginning to explore the movements of his body and his environment in his own individual way. As a result of her observations Jess was able to respond effectively to Angus and provide experiences that build on his actions and gestures.

TRY IT OUT

Provide babies with mirrors.

◆ Observe and make notes of how they explore what they look like.
◆ Make a note of their facial expressions, gestures and vocalisations.
◆ Look at the relevant component card, access the Birth to Three Matters CD-ROM and find out how children can develop a growing awareness of themselves.
◆ Think about what you have learned from this observation, how you could support the development of children, and make your practice more effective.

Being acknowledged and affirmed

This component focuses on how babies and young children need recognition, comfort and acceptance, and examines how they can contribute to relationships and explore emotional boundaries.

CASE STUDY

Charlotte is helping Wesley, aged 22 months, to wash his hands after painting. She crouches down so that she is at the same level as Wesley and can maintain eye contact. She then shows him how to turn on the tap, afterwards allowing him to do it for himself. While Wesley is washing his hands, Charlotte talks to him about what he is doing and praises his efforts. This helps Wesley understand that Charlotte values him and that he is important to her.

This case study shows that Charlotte provides the child with recognition, and makes them aware that they are important to her.

TRY IT OUT

Observe a key person with a child over a full session in a care setting, if possible.

◆ Make a note of how, when, why and where the key person praises the child (this could form part of your aim).
◆ Make a note of the child's responses (this could form part of your objective).
◆ You might find that an event sample is a suitable method of recording this information.
◆ You might want to consider how the key person responds to the child, whatever their personal feelings.
◆ Read about the work and research of Ainsworth, Elfer and Manning-Morton in the literature review found on the Birth to Three Matters CD-ROM. This should help you to develop your understanding. Consider how these researchers have built on the work of Bowlby.

This observation links to the component 'Being acknowledged and affirmed'.

Developing self-assurance

This component considers how children and babies gain self-assurance through close relationships and becoming confident in their own abilities.

THINK ABOUT IT

It is generally accepted by childcare professionals that a young child who has the opportunity to develop self-assurance will have better resources to cope with difficulties and challenges later in life. However, some people find that the need to protect a child from harm while providing opportunities to be responsible and independent very challenging and, on occasions, time consuming. For example, allowing a young child to pour their own drinks runs the risk of spillages. In the same way allowing a young child to dress themselves, such as putting on their own socks, will take longer than if an adult did it for them. However, with thoughtful planning it is achievable and will help the child to experience the joy of doing something for themselves, and therefore shows that the adult values and appreciates the child's abilities. It may mean that the adults in the setting will have to observe the routine of their day or session. As a result of their observations adults may make adjustments to allow time for the independent actions of the child.

CASE STUDY

A group of children between two and three years old have been playing outside with large blocks and planks. Before they tidy everything away the children and adult discuss how they can move some of the larger and heavier pieces of equipment. The adult observes the children decide that several people will have to work together to carry one plank.

This case study shows how the adult values the children's abilities and allows them to develop confidence in what they can do.

TRY IT OUT

Observe a child either attempting to dress themselves or feeding themselves.

◆ Make a note of their reactions when they succeed in the task, look at their body language, gestures, facial expressions, and verbal communication.

◆ Did the child have enough time to successfully complete the task?

◆ What was the adult doing while the child was attempting this task?

◆ Was the adult supportive of the child's efforts?

◆ Do there need to be any changes to routines or timings in the setting so that children can do things for themselves? If so, what changes would you recommend?

A sense of belonging

This component considers how babies and young children acquire social confidence and competencies. It also includes how children can develop a role and identity within a group.

Group play helps children develop a sense of identity

CASE STUDY

Matt is the key person in the toddler room of a day nursery. He makes sure that the young children in his care hang up their own face cloths in their own special place. He recognises that this will help to develop the young children's sense of belonging.

TRY IT OUT

Observe a group of children playing together.

◆ Make a note of social interaction within the group, particularly of what approaches or ways the children have to join in or avoid the play situation. (This could form part of an aim and the objective, but would need to include specific details of the group, such as gender, ages etc.)

◆ Look at the literature review on the Birth to Three Matters CD-ROM, in particular the research of Dunn and others to develop your understanding of how young children acquire social confidence.

This observation links to the component 'A sense of belonging'.

A skilful communicator

Refer to the pink cards in the Birth to Three Matters pack.

This aspect concentrates on the significance of young children being able to hear language and being able to respond to it. It is very important that the parents and key people in a baby's life respond appropriately to his/her experiments with sound, gestures and interactions. Babies will learn from the pleasurable responses of key people, such as smiles and facial expressions, and will be motivated to continue to communicate. Whilst small babies do not add as much to a conversation as adults might, early attempts at vocalisation do produce effective consequences. For example, babies are able to learn the 'rules' of conversation, such as turn-taking (I make a sound or gesture or facial expression and then wait, you respond and then wait for me to respond, and so on).

The four components of the aspect 'A skilful communicator' are:

◆ being together

◆ finding a voice

◆ listening and responding

◆ making meaning.

Being together

This component looks at how babies and young children become sociable and effective communicators. It includes ways of making contact, gaining attention and encouraging conversations. Being together reinforces the need for babies and children to develop positive relationships with each other and adults. Being close to a child and maintaining eye contact helps to establish relationships as well as promote language and communication. It can be difficult to keep up communication with another person who is close to you but who doesn't look at you!

CASE STUDY

A group of children aged between two years and two years seven months are in the role-play 'kitchen' playing with Rashda, a key person. Rashda makes the noise of a telephone ringing and says, 'Khalid, can you answer the phone please?' Khalid answers the phone and Rashda pretends to be the person on the other end. She has a conversation with Khalid. Khalid puts the phone down and turns to Daisy, 'mum will be late for dinner,' he says.

This case study shows that Rashda recognises the importance of becoming involved in children's play in order to stimulate their language development. It also supports the aspect of 'Being together' because the children and Rashda are using a variety of ways in which to communicate.

TRY IT OUT

Observe a group of children looking at and talking about books with an adult.

◆ Focus on how the children gain the attention of the adult (this could be the aim).

◆ Observe the ways that the adult encourages conversation, for example, what type of questions are asked?

◆ Find out more about the role of the adult or key person in supporting children becoming skilful communicators. Look at the views of theorists and researchers such as Vygotsky, Goldsmeid and Selleck. You can find more about this topic on the Birth to Three Matters CD-ROM.

Finding a voice

This component considers how babies and young children become confident and competent users of language. It looks at the fact that babies are sociable from birth and use a variety of ways to communicate. Babies need to be near familiar people and communicate in a variety of ways with them. It also considers how children use language to share their feelings, thought and experiences.

CASE STUDY

Jess cares for Angus, aged three months. Jess has observed several different cries that Angus uses to communicate his needs. She hears a distinct difference in the cries Angus makes when he is hungry from the cries he makes when he is tired, or is trying to get her attention. Having this knowledge means that Jess can respond appropriately to Angus.

TRY IT OUT

Listen to and observe the sounds and early 'words' a baby makes during a care routine such as nappy changing or feeding. (Select and make a note of the baby's age according to your own personal circumstances.)

◆ Observe the responses of the adult and try to assess opportunities for turn-taking and how the adult interprets the baby's attempts at communication.

◆ You may want to consider the work of Noam Chomsky and B.F. Skinner to widen your understanding of how children acquire language. The works of Vygotsky, Goldschmeid, Selleck, and Whitehead may also help you understand more about the role of the key person and adults in the development of language. Look on the Birth to Three Matters CD-ROM for more information on these researchers.

This observation links to the component 'Finding a voice'.

Jess recognises that 'Finding a voice' includes all forms of vocalisation so she also encourages Angus to respond to her by smiling, moving his arms and legs and making sounds.

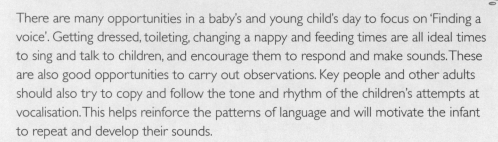

THINK ABOUT IT

There are many opportunities in a baby's and young child's day to focus on 'Finding a voice'. Getting dressed, toileting, changing a nappy and feeding times are all ideal times to sing and talk to children, and encourage them to respond and make sounds. These are also good opportunities to carry out observations. Key people and other adults should also try to copy and follow the tone and rhythm of the children's attempts at vocalisation. This helps reinforce the patterns of language and will motivate the infant to repeat and develop their sounds.

Listening and responding

Being a skilful communicator does not just involve talking – being able to listen and respond to what others say is just as important. Children need time to listen and respond to the sounds and communications that they see and hear, and sometimes adults do not give them enough time in which to do this. This

There is more to communication than just talking

component emphasises the importance of listening and responding appropriately to others, whatever form of language they are using.

Children with acute communication problems need to use non-verbal ways of making contact with others. They also need to know that their efforts are valued by others and that they are given time to respond.

CASE STUDY

Martha is three years old and was deprived of oxygen at birth so she has limited control over her body. When asked by her key person if she wanted water or milk to drink Martha is able to shake her head and keep her mouth closed to show her choice. Her key person waits for Martha's response before she says anything else, and then verbally acknowledges this choice.

Children who use English as a second language need to know that their home language is valued and should be encouraged to communicate in any way that they can. Gestures and body language may help a child grasp the meaning of a situation and provide opportunities for them to respond. Bilingual staff should feel comfortable about using more than one language with the children and babies. Singing songs and rhymes, and reacting to music can be universal.

CASE STUDY

In a large day nursery two members of staff lead a singing session. Nick sang a familiar rhyme in English and did all the actions, whereas Rashda, from Bangladesh, sang the same rhyme in Sylheti, again with all the actions. All the children were able to join in with either the actions or the words on both occasions.

TRY IT OUT

Try to observe the main carer/key person of a young child interacting with them, such as looking at a book or playing together.

- Observe the adult's response to the child's messages, such as responses to facial expressions, movements, actions, and vocalisations (this could be an aim).
- How does the adult respond, do they use language, facial expressions, body language, actions and movements?
- Research the work and ideas of Vygotsky, Bloom et al, and Dunn from the Birth to Three Matters CD-ROM to help develop your understanding of the importance of listening and responding.

Making meaning

This component looks at how babies and young children communicate meanings and influence others, it also considers how children learn to negotiate, make choices and understand each other. Allowing babies and children to make choices encourages then to negotiate, cooperate and problem solve. Choices can be numerous, for example, what to drink, whether to go outside or not, which colour to use when painting, where to sit, what to play with, what to do and so on. It also follows that if you encourage children to negotiate with you, there may be times when you will not be able to agree with their choices, and may even have to say no. Young children need to be given simple explanations as to why you cannot allow their choice. Sometimes role-play situations can be useful to help children resolve potential conflict situations and understand why their choice was not appropriate to that time and in that situation.

CASE STUDY

Gemma carried out the following observation in the pre-school group of Tomo, for whom the first language was Japanese.

Aim: to observe Tomo, a Japanese speaking boy aged two years and three months, making choices about what he eats.

Objective: to assess the effectiveness of picture cards and how Tomo makes his choices known.

Tomo sits at the table with an adult and three other children. The adult asks the children what they want to eat at snack time. She shows Tomo picture cards of toast and vegetable and fruit pieces, and asks him what he would like. Tomo points with his index finger to the card of fruit pieces. 'You would like fruit Tomo?' asks the adult while touching the card. Tomo nods his head and smiles. When the fruit pieces are put on the table he claps his hands together, smiles and nods his head.

Gemma looked at the work of Vygotsky, Baratt-Pugh (2000), Siraj-Blatchford (2000) and Whitehead (1996) to help her evaluate her findings and develop a greater understanding of bilingualism and how children make themselves understood.

TRY IT OUT

Carry out an observation of a group of young children engaged in role-play and/or dressing up.

- Observe how the children decide who will take on which roles, or wear dressing-up clothes.
- Think about ways the adult could support the children in negotiating and making choices.
- Find out about the research of Singer and others from the Birth to Three Matters CD-ROM, the Internet and books.

A *competent learner*

Refer to the green cards in the Birth to Three Matters pack.

The four components that make up this aspect are all interconnected. All relate to ways in which children make sense of the world in which they live. Babies and young children make sense of their world in many ways, including use of all of their senses and their whole being. It is through being given opportunities and becoming able to make marks, dance, draw, use words, movements, music and imaginative play that children share their thoughts, feelings and understanding.

The components of 'A competent learner' are:

◆ making connections

◆ being imaginative

◆ being creative

◆ representing.

Making connections

This component looks at ways that babies and young children use their senses and movements to make connections with their environment. This can mean becoming aware of patterns, sequences and classifications. It also considers how children become playfully occupied.

THINK ABOUT IT

Babies are ready to explore their world from the first moments after birth, but they need adults, and later on other children, to support and extend their explorations. Initially, a young baby appears to be fascinated with the human face. Studies have shown that babies prefer to look at shapes and patterns that resemble a human face than abstract designs. This means that it is possible for babies to make connections between what they see and the significant adults in their life. Babies use all of their senses to help them understand their world, for example, they will reach out and touch your hair and parts of your face. They will move up close to smell you and may explore further with their tongues and lips. We should never underestimate the power of the sensory exploration and how this stimulates physical movement.

CASE STUDY

In the video *Heuristic Play with Objects* (National Children's Bureau, 1992), children between 12 and 20 months are shown exploring everyday objects, such as large tins and cans, plastic tubes and bottles, pegs, jar lids, and egg boxes. The video shows a number of ways in which the various materials can be used, but the possibilities to provide young children with sensory experiences are endless. For instance, you can get them to make sequences, patterns and sort things into groups. The children in the video explore the materials in an open-ended way with no 'right' or 'wrong' result. Although the adults are present and close by, they remain quiet during the play session, but are obviously supportive through their gestures, facial expressions and body language.

TRY IT OUT

Try to do this observation with a baby who can sit unsupported, but who is not yet fully mobile. You can also do this activity with a baby who can be propped up safely with cushions or pillows.

◆ Put together a collection of natural objects, at least 20 different things, and place them in a basket.
◆ Put the basket on the floor and sit the baby alongside it.
◆ Allow the baby to explore the contents of the basket. You do not need to interact with the baby, it is sufficient to be within their vision, giving reassuring smiles and body movements to encourage them.
◆ You will need to develop your own aim and objective.
◆ Observe how the baby uses all of their senses to explore the objects.
◆ Observe other movements that the baby may make such as in their feet and toes.
◆ Observe how often the baby repeats an action. This could be linked to Piaget's theory of mastery play.
◆ You may want to read about the schema and research of Chris Athey to help you understand more about making connections.

This observation links to the components 'Making connections', 'Being imaginative' and 'Being creative'.

Being imaginative

This component looks at how babies and young children respond to the world, imitating, mirroring, exploring and re-enacting experiences. Have you ever noticed that sometimes when a baby or a young child is given a gift-wrapped present they spend as much time, if not more, exploring the gift-wrapping as they do the actual present? At such times these children are using all of their senses to play imaginatively with materials that are close at hand.

Bruner (1915) believed that play needs flexibility of thought, and provides opportunities to explore and experiment without limits. A sensitive adult who can provide a young child with opportunities and resources to meet this need without putting them under pressure to 'perform', will enable them to learn and develop in a safe and secure way. Remember, a caring and responsive adult is possibly the most valuable resource a child can have.

CASE STUDY

After a shopping trip to the supermarket with her parents, Emily, aged two years and three months, played with the large cardboard carton that had been used to carry some shopping. She sat in it, on it, crawled under it, put some of her toys in it, then she pushed it and pulled until it eventually fell apart. This is an example of imaginative play: Emily was able to explore using all her senses as well as engaging in pretend play. There was no pressure on Emily during this play so she was operating at a high level of learning.

This case study links to 'Being imaginative' as well as other components, such as 'Being creative'.

TRY IT OUT

There are many observations that can be carried out which would link to this aspect. A few of these are listed below, but you may think of others yourself.

◆ Provide real things for children to play with such as telephones and safe utensils from a real kitchen. For example, wooden spoons, pans, lids and plastic containers. Observe how the children imitate or mirror the actions of adults.

◆ Provide children with lengths of different textured materials to play with rather than dressing-up clothes. Observe how the children respond and how they use their senses while playing.

◆ Observe the words and language that the children use in their imaginative play. See if you can link these words to their learning and other aspects and components of the Birth to Three Matters framework, such as 'Making meaning' and 'Finding a voice'.

◆ Provide babies with items that make noises or move such as simple percussion instruments or simple push-along toys. Observe how the baby responds to the sounds and movements.

Being creative

This component is also about the children exploring and discovering, having opportunities to experiment whilst at the same time gaining in confidence and competence. The last suggestion for an observation in the Try it out box above could also link to this aspect because an observation could be made of the sounds

Experimental play encourages
creativity

and movements a baby makes as they explore. Tina Bruce explores the creative
process in *Cultivating Creativity* (2004). Bruce believes that creativity is, like play,
a very complex notion that can be described as stage-like. Adults need to develop
understanding of the creative process if they are to support babies and young
children.

CASE STUDY

Laura observed a group of children from 18 months to two years old while they
were painting. The objective of her observation was to assess the level of adult
support and involvement in the activity. Laura noticed that the adult talked to them
about what they were doing, but made no attempt to show the children how to hold
the paintbrushes properly. Laura thought that perhaps the adult should have done
this and in her recommendations she wrote that the adult could have become more
involved with the children, and shown them how to hold the brushes. However, when
discussing this with her tutor, Laura realised that the adult was allowing the children to
experiment and try out the brushes for themselves. This allowed them to be creative,
resourceful and develop competencies by themselves. Laura decided that she had
quite a lot to write in the 'personal learning' section of this observation.

TRY IT OUT

Observe young children experimenting and exploring with 'messy' play materials, such as fingerpaint, cornflour and water, and shaving foam.

◆ Observe the facial expressions of the children as they explore and play.
◆ Observe what support, if any, young children may require.
◆ Consider how an adult could extend and develop these sensory experiences.
◆ Research the concept of schemas – see the Birth to Three Matters CD-ROM.
◆ Look at the work of Tina Bruce on the creative process.

Representing

The component of representing looks closely at how young children make marks and symbols to help them explore and develop their understanding of the world. For example, many parents and carers notice that their young children can differentiate between the plastic bags of major supermarkets, even though the child cannot read the name printed on the bag. They can recognise the symbols and give them meaning and identity.

It is good practice to provide babies and young children with lots of opportunities to make marks in a range of different contexts. For example, having paper and writing materials in the role-play corner, having sticks and tools that can be used in wet sand to make marks, or encouraging children to fingerpaint over a large smooth surface. All of these situations would provide good opportunities for observing children's reactions, behaviour and development. Young babies usually find out about mark-marking by accident – they may spill some food onto the tray of their chair and make marks as they move their fingers through the food. It can sometimes be hard for adults to value these early mark-making attempts, especially when it is all so messy.

CASE STUDY

Dan (an adult), and George, aged two years and five months, are painting together. George is talking to Dan as he paints his dad's car. He talks about the wheels and colour of the car, and then tells Dan where he sits and paints himself in the car. To an outsider George's painting does not look like a conventional representation of a car, but Dan values George's attempts to tell him about his painting and his personal representation of a familiar experience. He asks open-ended questions and uses lots of verbal praise of George's attempts to represent his ideas and feelings.

TRY IT OUT

Mix up some cornflour and water on a firm surface or tray. Allow a baby to move their fingers through the mixture. Watch and make a note of their reactions.

- Do they make sounds and attempts at vocalisation?
- Observe their facial expressions, gestures and body language.
- Do they repeat the same actions? If so what does this tell you?
- Does the child gain in self-assurance and experiment and explore with confidence?
- Link this observation to other components of the framework, such as 'Being imaginative', 'Developing self-assurance', and 'Finding a voice'.
- Look on the Birth to Three Matters CD-ROM for information to help you develop your understanding of how children represent their experiences.

This component also considers how babies and young children can begin to understand that sometimes one object or symbol can represent something else, for example a plastic banana can become a telephone in a role-play situation, just as a carton can become a truck or car. This understanding comes through play and reinforces how children make sense of their world through imaginative and creative play activities in which they can take the lead, make choices and satisfy their natural curiosity. Piaget recognised the value of play and symbolism (the ability to make one thing represent something else), is a feature of his cognitive development theory. There are many researchers, such as Tina Bruce and Janet Moyles, who have studied children's play and the impact on cognitive development.

TRY IT OUT

Read the following extract from an observation and try to draw some conclusions that would support the aspect of 'A competent learner'.

Think about how Harry makes connections and represents his experiences of the world.

Research current theories about how children learn through play from the Birth to Three Matters CD-ROM.

Aim: to observe Harry (two years old) in the role-play area.

Objective: To assess his responses to imaginative play and opportunities to discover that one thing can stand for another.

Harry pretends to make a cup of coffee using plastic cups and a large box which he calls the kettle. He pretends to switch the kettle on by pressing a button on the side of the box. 'Nearly ready,' he says. He pretends to put coffee in the cup and pour the water. He turns to the adult, 'coffee's done,' he says. Harry gives a cup to the adult and then picks up a doll. He sits down on a chair and pretends to give the doll a drink. He blows on the cup and says 'hot.'

A *healthy child*

Refer to the blue cards in the Birth to Three Matters pack.

This aspect is about much more than just physical health, and, as with the previous aspects 'A healthy child' is inter-related to all of the others, in this case bringing together mental and physical well-being. Meeting a baby's and young child's physical needs is essential to their overall well-being. Growing children who are physically healthy have the energy and interest to explore their environment and become involved in activities planned for them. Emotional health is also fundamental. Babies and young children need to feel that they are special, and that they can confidently express their feelings and develop ways of dealing with potentially stressful situations.

THINK ABOUT IT

Margaret McMillan put equal importance on children's health, social care and their educational development. She is attributed with starting the first school clinic in 1908 and, along with her sister, founded an open-air nursery school in 1914. The aim of this school was to meet physical, health and educational needs of disadvantaged children. Today, the SureStart initiatives are following McMillan's lead with integrated approaches to nursery education, health and social issues, and involving a multi-professional team in order to meet the needs of babies, young children and their families.

Abraham Maslow's hierarchy of needs was developed in the 1960s. He suggested that there are universal needs which every human strives to satisfy. If our needs are not met or satisfied, the consequences will have an impact on every aspect of our development. The aspect of a healthy child is about meeting the basic needs in many respects, in that rest and sleep, food, shelter, and security are vital for emotional and physical well-being.

Find out more about Maslow's hierarchy of needs. It will help you understand children's development more fully and will enable links to be made between theory and practice.

Feeding times are key experiences for babies and young children and are not just for providing nourishment. These times can provide learning opportunities to build close attachments with a key person and can help the child develop language, cognitive and social skills. This is also true of nappy changing times, toileting sessions and other care routines. In all of these situations there are endless opportunities for non-verbal and verbal exchanges between an adult and child. The video provided with the Birth to Three Matters pack has a short clip of an excellent interchange between a childcare practitioner and a young boy during nappy changing.

Aim: to observe a baby or child during feeding time or nappy changing (choose the age appropriate to your setting).

Objective: to assess the verbal and non-verbal exchanges and expressions of feeling between the adult and the child or baby.

Think about the frequency of the exchanges and expressions.

Who initiates these exchanges – the baby, child, or the adult?

Link this to your understanding of the importance of a key person, discussed earlier in this chapter.

The components of 'A healthy child' are:

◆ growing and developing

◆ keeping safe

◆ emotional well-being

◆ healthy choices.

Growing and developing

The component of growing and developing focuses on children being well-nourished and acquiring physical skills, but also on opportunities to be active, rested and safe. Rest and sleep are as necessary to babies and young children as their diet. Quite often behaviour will change when a baby or young child is tired and it is important that caring adults recognise the signs of tiredness.

CASE STUDY

Sara is a nanny in a private family for twin girls, both of whom are one year old. Sara observes that both girls become less cooperative when tired, one girl even becomes quite stubborn and will refuse to do what she asks of her. The other girl can become tearful and fractious. Sara has learned to become aware of these signs and provides opportunities for the girls to rest and sleep before the situation develops into a potential clash. They might sit together quietly looking at a book, or watching a DVD, sometimes they snuggle up together on the sofa and listen to quiet music.

Growing and developing focuses on acquiring physical skills, including large and fine motor movement. Young children need lots of opportunities to develop large muscle skills such as walking, jumping and climbing, and also fine motor skills such as feeding themselves, fastening buttons and zips, as well as holding mark-marking tools.

Fine motor skills like pouring improve quickly with practice and encouragement

TRY IT OUT

Read the following extract from a checklist observation which has been done in a day nursery setting.

Aim: to look at the fine motor skills of a group of children aged between two years three months and two years seven months.

Objective: to assess fine motor skills development in order to plan appropriate activities that will meet individual needs.

Key
X: not achieved　　✓: achieved

Fine motor skill	Girl A	Girl B	Boy C	Boy D
Feeds themselves using a spoon	X	✓	X	✓
Feeds themselves with a fork	X	X	X	✓
Can pull up a zip on their coat	✓	✓	✓	✓
Can fasten buttons	X	X	X	✓
Can pour a drink	✓	✓	✓	✓

Note that this is only a partial checklist. More information on developmental norms can be found in the chart at the end of this book.

From the information that you can see, what conclusion can you draw about the following.

◆ The skill development of the children according to the developmental norms or milestones set out in the table.

◆ The opportunities in the setting for the children to develop fine motor skills.

◆ The method of the observation. Think about the advantages and disadvantages of comparing development in this way, and the information that is missing, such as the length of time taken to 'achieve' the task, as well as the role of the adult.

◆ What activities could you plan to meet the individual needs of these children?

Try to carry out an observation using a different method, where you can assess a specific feature of the physical development of a young child, such as hand-eye coordination, balance, and fine motor skills.

Think about how this information can be used to plan activities and experiences that support this child's development.

Keeping safe

Part of being safe and protected is about discovering boundaries and limits, knowing about rules, when to seek help and when to say no. Children need to know who they can ask for help, especially as their need for love and affection can make them vulnerable. It is good practice to plan activities and experiences which help to teach them who to ask for assistance and help.

A fundamental role for practitioners working with children is the responsibility to keep them safe. This includes being in a safe environment, understanding child protection issues and helping children to become aware of dangers and risks to their well-being. There is always the risk that some adults may become over-protective of children and this can restrict the child's ability to learn how to protect themselves. However, it is important to remember that over-protectiveness should not be mistaken for concern about a child, and it is better to speak out to another adult about any concerns, even if they turn out to be unfounded.

CASE STUDY

A parent of a child in pre-school was very protective of her daughter. She was very concerned about the child each day she left her at pre-school, spending a long time settling her. The parent always insisted on coming with her daughter on trips or walks outside of the setting. The child had suffered complications at birth, resulting in an extended stay in hospital. While the staff could understand the parent's concerns they also realised that the child's learning was being affected as she lacked confidence and was very reluctant to try anything new. As the parent was well known, staff found it relatively easy to discuss the impact that this over-protectiveness was having on the child. They did not expect the parent to change overnight but she did agree to shorten the time that she spent settling her child and so allow the girl to make her own choices about what she played with.

TRY IT OUT

Observe a baby or young child over a whole morning or afternoon if possible.

◆ Observe how they let the adult know what they want and need, including help, for example, to get out of a feeding chair.

◆ You may find that an event sample is a suitable method of recording this information.

◆ How can this information be linked to planning experiences and activities for this child?

◆ Look on the Birth to Three Matters CD-ROM for information about meeting needs.

Emotional well-being

This component focuses on how babies and young children need to feel special to someone, how they learn to express their feelings and develop independence, as well as recognising when they need to be dependent upon others. The role of the key person has already been discussed earlier in this chapter, but its importance is re-emphasised here. Babies and young children not only need, but actively seek out opportunities to become close to a key person. It is vitally important that care settings and parents establish procedures to exchange information about the baby and young child's well-being. Some settings use home/nursery diaries, others informally exchange information when the child is handed over at the start and end of each session. The method is not as important as the fact that it happens, which helps babies and young children understand that there are adults who care for them and are concerned about their well-being.

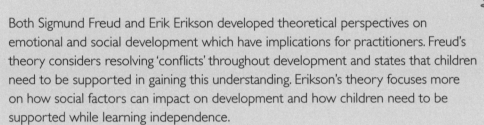

CASE STUDY

One inner city nursery has all the email addresses of the parents. The key person has the responsibility of sending an email to parents of the children in their care each week to give an overview of what has happened in the nursery. Parents are asked to send one back to the nursery at the start of the week to let the staff know about significant events over the weekend. The emails supplement daily informal exchanges between the key people and the parents, and the daily record sheet of nappy changing, rest, sleep and food is given to parents at the end of the session.

THINK ABOUT IT

Both Sigmund Freud and Erik Erikson developed theoretical perspectives on emotional and social development which have implications for practitioners. Freud's theory considers resolving 'conflicts' throughout development and states that children need to be supported in gaining this understanding. Erikson's theory focuses more on how social factors can impact on development and how children need to be supported while learning independence.

Adults sometimes find it difficult to express and communicate their emotions to others. We place great reliance on facial expressions and body language to express our feelings, rather than spoken word, and may expect others to interpret the messages we send correctly. When others misinterpret facial expressions and body language we can feel hurt and misunderstood. Babies and young children are not yet able to speak about their feelings, needs and wants, and so have to use facial expressions, cries and body language. It is therefore of vital importance that practitioners learn to recognise and correctly interpret these messages. This can be done with sensitive observations and practice.

TRY IT OUT

Observe a baby or young child with their key person or parent engaged in an affectionate interchange.

◆ Note the facial expressions, body language and sounds of the child responding to the adult.
◆ Note how the adult responds to the child's messages.
◆ Research around the subject of relationships and emotional development to extend your understanding of how to meet the child's needs.

Healthy choices

Babies and young children need to learn how to make choices and this is the focus of the component 'Healthy choices'. Making choices includes finding out about their bodies, what they are capable of, and what they can do. It is also about being able to show preferences, likes and dislikes, making decisions, and becoming more aware of others and their needs. Sometimes this can present us with challenges, for example, how would you react when a child has made a choice that you consider to be unhealthy, such as eating certain foods or playing with certain toys?

CASE STUDY

Jordan, aged two years and four months, attends a pre-school group for three sessions each week. He prefers to play with the dressing-up clothes and frequently puts on a pink 'fairy' outfit. The staff recognise that it is important for them to provide opportunities for children to make choices, but one or two find it difficult to accept Jordan's choice of play attire and feel that it is inappropriate. The whole staff team talk about this and accept that Jordan has a right to make his own choices, even though some staff do not agree. It is decided that his well-being is not being threatened; he is playing safely and cooperatively, he shares and rarely gets into conflict situations with other children.

TRY IT OUT

Observe a group of children making choices. This could be done as they come into the setting and see the range of activities and experiences set out for them. Choose your age group as appropriate to your setting.

◆ Observe the choices that the children make, and also the things that they choose not to do.
◆ You could do this observation using the tracking method, perhaps colour coding for different children? However, the main disadvantage of using this method is that you will have to be very neat or your observation could be hard to check later.
◆ You could try recording this information in a table, for example:

Chosen by	Activity 1	Activity 2	Activity 3	Activity 4	Activity 5	Activity 6
Child A						
Child B						
Child C						
Child D						
Child E						

Alternatively, you could use a narrative or written method.

Throughout the Birth to Three Matters Framework the importance of a supportive adult is repeatedly mentioned. Exploring boundaries, making choices and decisions require the support of a responsive adult. Babies and young children who have developed secure attachments to key people in the early stages of their lives are more able to cope with problem solving situations and any problems that they may confront later on. Adults need to think about the ways that they can support babies and young children in learning how to make choices. One way that they can do this is to develop their own understanding of the importance of the adult's role through reading and researching about attachments, and ways to support children and their families in developing attachments.

In conclusion, it must be remembered that the Birth to Three Matters Framework is not a curriculum, but is there to act as supportive guidance. It is not intended to be a series of topics or developmental areas on which to base planning. The success of using the framework depends on the adults following it, their observations, subsequent planned activities and the experiences offered to the children. It encourages and promotes a holistic approach to caring for children and supporting their development. Practitioners need to be committed to developing effective relationships with the children in their care. They also need to be committed to developing their own understanding and knowledge about all aspects of a child's development and must keep up-to-date with current research and views. Adults need to perceive observations as a fundamental part of their practice, supporting babies and young children while they grow and develop.

Chapter 7 Linking observations to the Foundation Stage Curriculum

The Foundation Stage Curriculum, or the curriculum for children before statutory school age, begins the term after a child's third birthday. It was introduced in September 2000 and guidance published by QCA in the same year is used to support it.

The curriculum is divided into six areas of learning and early learning goals (ELGs). These are:

◆   personal, social and emotional development

◆   communication, language and literacy

◆   mathematical development

◆   knowledge and understanding of the world

◆   physical development

◆   creative development.

(In Wales children currently follow the Desirable Learning Outcomes and in Northern Ireland the Curricular Guidance for Pre-school Education is used.)

The actual headings may vary slightly between England, Scotland, Wales and Northern Ireland, but the content is broadly similar. However, The Welsh Assembly is piloting 'The Learning Country' during the academic year of 2004/05, which proposes that children do not start the National Curriculum and Key Stage 1 until Year 2, thus enabling them to stay within a play-based curriculum for longer.

As one of the principles for early years education in *Curriculum guidance for the Foundation Stage* (2000) QCA states that 'practitioners must be able to observe and respond appropriately to children, informed by acknowledgement of how children develop and learn and a clear understanding of possible next steps in their development and learning'. The information from numerous and frequent observations of what children have said or done can be gathered in a variety of ways. Talking to children, observing them, and looking at the outcomes of activities are all valuable ways to gain an insight of what children know, understand and can do.

The Foundation Stage Curriculum sets early learning goals as guidance for practitioners

As mentioned previously in this book, practitioners must carry out frequent observations of children in order to build a complete picture of their development. This is especially important in the foundation stage because particular areas of a child's development can be met through more than one area of learning. For example, a child can develop turn-taking skills while playing in a role-play area, but the same skills can also be developed while talking and listening to others. Similarly, one activity can provide numerous learning opportunities, for example, painting can provide opportunities to be creative, develop physical skills, language skills, and expressing feelings just to mention a few. There may be occasions when it is appropriate to have a specific aim for an observation, such as when a particular area of a child's learning has been identified as needing further support. On the other hand it may be more appropriate at certain times to carry out holistic observations, such as in the examples of activities given above.

This chapter will:

◆ give a brief overview of the Foundation Stage Curriculum guidance and profile

◆ look at how observations can support and develop practice within each of the six areas of learning.

A *brief overview of the foundation stage*

The foundation stage begins when children reach the age of three and it aims to underpin all future learning. The curriculum guidance identifies stepping stones that show the knowledge, skills, understanding and attitudes that children should develop and learn during the foundation stage in order to achieve each of the six ELGs. The stepping stones are not related to age but are progressive, and practitioners can use them to help plan appropriate activities and experiences. They can also be used as assessment tools to inform observations.

In September 2003 the Foundation Stage Profile was introduced. It is a single national assessment system for the foundation stage and replaces the various baseline assessment schemes that were previously in use throughout England. It builds on the guidance and sets out a way of summarising children's achievements. It also provides very useful information for parents and teachers in Year 1, having 13 summary scales which cover all six areas of learning that should be completed by the time a child begins Key Stage 1. The main purpose of this assessment is to work out the level of attainment achieved by each child in each of the six areas of learning. This assessment is underpinned by a range of frequent, sensitive observations of children throughout the foundation stage.

Personal, social and emotional development

Personal, social and emotional development is of vital importance to the overall development of young children. Successful development in this area will impact on all other areas of learning. It covers knowing who you are, where you fit in, feeling respect for others, having social competencies and emotional well-being. The example, or role model, of the childcare and education worker is very important in making children feel secure and helping them to develop skills and attitudes. Children learn to trust and feel emotionally safe and secure when they have consistent key adults to relate to.

Early years practitioners have a very important part to play in helping young children understand their emotions and how to manage strong feelings. It is not really possible to separate emotional development from other areas of development, because everything is inter-related. Very young children find it hard to manage their emotions and feelings so it is very important that practitioners understand how to support them. Some children have genetic disorders or learning difficulties that can affect aspects of their development, for example, they may not have developed strong and secure relationships or attachments and this may affect how they show emotion.

The Foundation Stage Profile assesses this area of learning in three different aspects:

◆ dispositions and attitudes

◆ social development

◆ emotional development.

CASE STUDY

Dawn is watching three children playing in the water tray. She observes that Charlie, who is standing nearby, is watching and smiling while the others play. Dawn encourages Charlie to join in and after a few moments he starts to play with the other children. One of the children asks Charlie to hold a piece of hosepipe so that she can pour water through it.

In this case study Dawn observed Charlie and correctly interpreted that he wanted to join in, but needed encouragement from her to do so. This observation would provide some evidence for Dawn that could contribute to Charlie's profile but it would also help her build a holistic picture of Charlie's development throughout the foundation stage.

TRY IT OUT

◆ Observe how a child shows personal independence, such as putting on outdoor clothes, washing their hands or pouring out their own drinks. You could link the information of this observation to the stepping stones and/or developmental milestones, then suggest activities that you could plan to promote future development.

◆ Observe how a child reacts and responds to new activities, look at their level of confidence and see if they initiate new ideas themselves. Think about how the adult could support and encourage confidence in children. Look at the work of Bruner and Vygotsky on how the adult, or other children, can support and extend learning and development.

◆ Observe the concentration levels of a group of children listening to a story or a visitor talking. This observation could consider the suitability of the activity, especially if the children do not concentrate, or ways in which children learn socially acceptable behaviour, such as sitting quietly while someone else is talking.

THINK ABOUT IT

Bruner states that adults can support children's emotional and social development by being actively involved with them, and used the term 'scaffolding'. He also believed that older children can 'scaffold' development by, for example, helping a younger child tidy away resources. Vygotsky emphasised the importance of social and cultural factors in a child's development, but also suggested that all children had potential which could be 'unlocked' by sensitive adults. He called this the zone of proximal development (ZPD).

The area of learning, personal, social and emotional development considers how the children play alongside and with others, how they build relationships, learning to share and take turns. It also looks at how children begin to understand the different needs and values of other people, and the need for agreed values and codes of behaviour. These areas of development are assessed by using information gathered through frequent observations from the beginning of the foundation stage, which in turn build on the child's earliest experiences and their progression in these areas as they mature, and are identified in the stepping stones. The stepping stones also give examples of how the adult can support the child's learning, not only in this area of learning but in all six areas of learning.

Read the following extract from a written observation, and then think about the questions that follow. The adults in the setting had particular concerns about how the children took turns and shared, they therefore developed specific aims and objectives. Their aim was to look at three children aged between three years seven months and four years of age playing in the role-play area. The objective was to assess how the children took turns and shared the resources.

Child A is watching children B and C in the role-play corner, they are looking through the dressing-up box. Child A goes over to join them, she picks up a length of material and puts it over her head, 'look,' she says, 'I'm a queen'. Child B and child C smile at her and start to hunt through the box for pieces of material. Child B finds a length of material and copies child A. 'There are two queens now,' she says. Child C is still looking in the box, but can't find any similar material. 'I want some,' she says'. Child C moves towards child A and grabs the material off her head, 'I want it now' says child C, child A shouts 'No, it's mine'. Child A and child C start to fight over the material. At this point an adult intervenes.

Think about the following points.

1. Can you match the development shown in this observation to the stepping stones for personal, social and emotional development, and/or developmental norms/milestones? What does this indicate about the children's development and needs?
2. What could this extract possibly indicate about the resources available to the children?
3. What do you think the adult should do to manage the behaviour and support the children's needs, development and learning?

Body language and facial expressions can say a lot to a competent observer

◆ Look at the photograph above.

◆ Look at the children's facial expressions, body language and gestures.

◆ What makes you think that these children are playing together amicably?

◆ Remember that a photograph is just a snapshot of a moment in the activity and two seconds later these children could be looking very different. While a child's body language, expressions and gestures are all important aspects of an observation, it should be remembered that several observations must be carried out before the evidence can really be beyond question.

TRY IT OUT

◆ Observe a group of children talking to an adult about right and wrong, such as why they should not hurt anyone, or words that they should or should not use when talking to each other. Listen to the children's suggestions and see if you can deduce anything about their understanding of right and wrong. You might want to link this information to the theories of Kohlberg and Piaget, both of whom looked at how children develop moral reasoning. Also, Erikson's theory of emotional development identifies distinct stages and considers how relationships with adults can influence a child's attitude to moral issues.

◆ Observe a child who is new to the setting but separated from their main carer. Think about the role of the key person or adults in managing this situation. Research the work of Emerson and Schaffer, or Bowlby, to help you understand attachment theory, separation anxiety, and how these can affect children's holistic development.

◆ Observe a group of children talking about significant personal events, such as Eid, a birthday, a wedding, having their bedroom decorated, getting something new, or the death of a pet. Note how children listen to each other and talk about their feelings. Try to link this to the stepping stones.

Personal, emotional and social development underpins all areas of development. It is therefore vital that everyone working with children is able to plan appropriate activities and experiences that will support their development and enable them to acquire a positive awareness of themselves.

Communication, language and literacy

Children need opportunities to use language and communication in all areas of their development and learning, so it is important that they are in an environment which encourages opportunities to extend their language skills. Children also need access to printed material in a variety of different formats, and to recognise print as a means of communication. We must also give children opportunities to listen and be listened to as they talk about their experiences. They will naturally be quiet in some activities and more talkative in others. For instance, they may be quiet when looking at books or listening to a story, and loud when playing in a sandpit. With support children will begin to learn different uses of language, such as asking questions, describing activities, experiences and feelings, negotiating with others, retelling and recalling events. Confidence and motivation play an important part in this area of learning. It is important that children get as many of these experiences as possible to encourage the positive use of the unstructured times when children communicate and use language. Planning is intrinsically linked to sensitive and informed observations.

Many children speak more than one language, and it has been suggested that children who are learning to use more than one language at the same time are slightly slower in learning to communicate and talk because they are thinking about more than one language system. In order for multilingual and bilingual children to develop their home or first language they must be supported and valued. Speaking another language can be part of a child's self-identity, so if their home or first language is not valued and supported, the child is being given the idea that the key person is not concerned about the culture or family of the child.

THINK ABOUT IT

There are several theorists who have studied language acquisition and development. Vygotsky and Bruner both suggested that there are links between a child's cognitive, or intellectual, development and language. Their work supported the 'nurture' view that language development is primarily influenced by the environment, social and cultural factors. On the other hand, Noam Chomsky believed that we are genetically programmed to learn language and coined the phrase Language Acquisition Device (LAD), suggesting that babies are born with an inbuilt facility for language. Chomsky therefore took the 'nature' standpoint, that language development is influenced primarily by genetic factors. However, in reality both nature and nurture contribute to development. Children experience language from birth and from a very early age become familiar with written signs and symbols in their environment. For example, many young children can identify the 'M' of McDonalds and know what it means even though they can't say the letter.

Communication, language and literacy can be observed in several ways, some of which are listed below.

◆ Written observations, but you might miss something that is said by gestures made or body language while you write. It is good practice to write up observation notes as soon as possible after the actual observation.

◆ Event samples are useful as you can record what a child says on specific occasions such as when playing with another child or in a new situation. Event samples may also be quite specific and can be used when occasions are clearly identified beforehand, and then observed whenever that particular event or behaviour occurs.

◆ Time samples can be used to record what a child says at regular intervals throughout the day or session, such as for five minutes every hour during a morning session.

◆ Checklists can be used to record specific features of language and communication such as vocabulary and sentence construction. Consideration would have to be given to the construction of the checklist and the stepping stones would be a useful tool.

- Audio recording can be made and then transcribed. The information and evidence of other observations could then be assessed using the stepping stones.

- Video recordings are useful as they show language, facial expressions and body language.

- Examples of children's writing and other mark-making are valuable ways of gathering information.

THINK ABOUT IT

From the suggested list above, select at least three different methods of observing children. Try to do at least one observation for each selected method.

Try to make a judgement on which method gave the most useful information for the aim. Is it possible to deduce why that method was successful, and what the advantages and disadvantages were?

The Foundation Stage Profile assesses this area of learning in four different aspects:

- language for communication and thinking

- linking sounds and letters

- reading

- writing.

These can be assessed in many different ways, as discussed above, but by asking the child open-ended questions it is possible to accumulate a huge amount of information. Questions and discussions can be formulated along the following lines:

- Giving a running commentary on what the child is doing and leaving an opening for them to bring in their own contributions. In doing this the adult is also supporting the child's vocabulary development as they give their commentary.

- 'I saw you in the water tray this morning, it looked so interesting. I saw you…' Children of this age often find it difficult to remember what activities they have been involved with and will need prompts to tell their 'story'.

- 'I have seen you looking at this book lots of times. Why is this your favourite story?'.

◆ 'What interesting writing, what does it say?'

◆ 'What do you think is going to happen next?'

By recording or making a note of the children's responses it is possible to learn a great deal about their communication, language and literacy development.

TRY IT OUT

◆ Ask children some of the questions above and start a discussion with them (you could use some of your own questions). Use their responses as supporting evidence for your observations.

◆ Did you lead the child in any way? Children of this age will need prompts to remember activities, but leading a child is different. It is when the adult suggests things for the child to say, for example, 'Is this your favourite story because you like where the dog lives?'.

◆ Did they say what they thought you wanted to hear? For example, during a circle time children have been observed repeating what the first child said, because the first child had got a positive response from the adult other children thought that it would also work for them. How could this affect your observations?

Children will use some form of communication in all areas of learning. Practitioners must be aware of how to support this essential aspect of development and learning, and should help children become confident enough to use language and different forms of communication in a variety of ways. This can be done through sensitive and appropriate planning using evidence from observations.

Mathematical development

This area of learning includes counting, sorting, matching, becoming aware of patterns, making connections, recognising relationships and working with numbers, shapes, space and measures. All of these aspects of mathematics can be developed through play and the opportunities

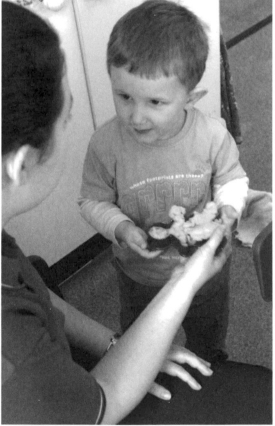

Playdough can provide good opportunities for promoting mathematical development

for observations are boundless. The Foundation Stage Profile specifically considers the following aspects:

◆ numbers as labels and for counting
◆ calculating
◆ shape, space and measures.

CASE STUDY

At the end of a play session the childcare and education worker sits on the carpet with a group of children. They sing familiar rhymes and songs together for about five minutes. Later that session Amir goes over to the music table, picks up a jingle ring and starts singing, 'One, two, three four five, once I caught a fish alive'. The adult observes this and makes a mental note that Amir can say some number names in familiar contexts, but also makes a note to carry out further observations to check that Amir can actually say number names correctly in other contexts and situations.

TRY IT OUT

◆ Observe a group of children playing with playdough and cutters. Observe the opportunities that they have to count and use numbers during the activity. Try and link this observation to theories and perspectives on how children learn, such as those by Piaget, Vygotsky, Donaldson, and Athey. Refer to the stepping stones to plan activities that could extend the children's learning.
◆ Do an event sample during a play session to observe and record how often a child uses numbers and counts in everyday situations and routines. Make a note of the context of use and try to link this information to how children can learn through firsthand experiences and the stepping stones.
◆ Observe a child playing with number cards or small scale numbered toys. Can the child put the numbers in the correct order? This observation can be linked to theoretical perspectives on how children learn, such as the work of Piaget and others mentioned above. Refer to the stepping stones to consider future activities.

THINK ABOUT IT

Singing provides many valuable learning opportunities for children to develop mathematical skills. For example, in addition to the case study above, rhymes where children count down such as 'Five currant buns' or 'Five speckled frogs' provide opportunities to use language associated with addition and subtraction. It is good practice to make a collection of the songs and rhymes that you can use with children which could help develop their mathematical understanding. Many of these have actions that provide children with visual prompts to help them remember the words. If you come across a rhyme or song that doesn't have actions, why not work some out with the children?

CASE STUDY

Read the following extract from a written observation of Toby, an NVQ Level 3 candidate working in a day nursery. Toby is observing a group of four children between three years four months and three years seven months in the role-play area. His aim was to observe the use of mathematical language in role-play, and the objective was to assess opportunities to use language associated with addition and subtraction. Toby intended to use this observation as assessment for his NVQ and realised that he would have to carry out more than one observation to fully assess the use of language in this context.

A, B, C and D are in the role-play kitchen, and are 'making' dinner.

A: 'get me some potatoes please C.'

C: 'how many do you want?'

A: '4 please.'

B: 'are there any left?'

C counts the potatoes and speaks, 'you want four so there will be two left'.

D starts to lay the table with four place settings. She counts out the plates, 'we need one more plate, we only have three. We have too many forks, we have one, two, three, four, five!'.

A starts to put the potatoes on the plates, 'we have some left,' she says.

D answers, 'that is because we don't have enough plates, we need some more'.

Using your knowledge and understanding of developmental milestones and norms, and the stepping stones, what conclusions could you draw from this short extract?

What recommendations would you make with regard to the planning of appropriate activities to meet the needs of these children?

Can you think of four open-ended questions that Toby could ask the children to extend their understanding and provide further evidence for his observation?

The third aspect of the Foundation Stage Profile assessment for mathematics is shape and space. Many practitioners use language to support this aspect of mathematics without really being aware if it, for example when talking about the shape of the paving stones, the doors, or the windows. Phrases such as 'under, over, in front of, behind, longer, shorter,' become part of everyday conversations.

Try to make a note of the number of times that you use such mathematical language with children in one hour. This could be recorded as a chart with the most frequently used words, or as an event sample.

TRY IT OUT

◆ Observe children at 'tidy-up' time. Make a note if any children have difficulties fitting items into boxes with lids to the extent at which the lids can be closed. What recommendations would you make using your evidence? Try to link this observation to theoretical ideas or schemas.

◆ Observe a child making a model with recycled materials. Make notes on the language used to describe the shapes of the materials. How could this data be used for assessing the child's needs?

◆ Observe a child sorting objects. Ask the child if they are sorting the objects in any particular way, such as colour, size or shape, or maybe just because they prefer some objects to others? Think about Vygotsky's ideas on play and developing skills. Look at the stepping stones as ways that this child's needs and development can be met in the future.

◆ Using the stepping stones, plan an activity that would encourage children to make patterns and sequences, such as threading beads of particular colours, or printing. Observe how many children can make simple repeating patterns. Use this data and the stepping stones to plan future activities that will extend the children's learning. This observation may encourage you to look at theoretical perspectives about memory such as those of Robert Case (1985).

THINK ABOUT IT

Robert Case is frequently portrayed as a neo-Piagetian because he merges aspects of Piaget's theory with information processing concepts. Information processing theorists believe that the mind is like a digital computer in that it uses a system of symbols and works to certain rules. Humans break down 'problems' into a series of simpler steps in the same way that a computer operates. An important part of any computer is the memory, and in the same way the human mind relies upon memory in order to learn and develop.

As with the previous areas of learning, confidence is the essential ingredient to successful understanding and learning. Confident children are motivated, keen and interested in learning. Children need to be presented with mathematical situations in a variety of formats such as songs and rhymes, role-play, stories, games and imaginative play so that they can develop their skills and understanding without fear of failure or non-achievement.

Knowledge and understanding of the world

It is through the activities and experiences contained within this area of the foundation stage that children learn how to make sense of the world in which they live. They also learn through observing the activities of others and this area of learning can provide many effective opportunities for children to satisfy their curiosity. Knowledge and understanding of the world lays the foundations for later activities in science, history, geography, and information and communication technology. It is very important, as with all areas of learning, that practitioners provide activities based upon firsthand experiences which encourage the children to explore, problem solve, ask questions and develop the skills of prediction, decision-making, discussion and critical thinking.

CASE STUDY

The children in a nursery class are involved in a topic about themselves. They have been asked to bring in photographs of themselves as babies. These are all displayed on the wall and the children find the pictures a source of great interest. They talk about how they looked as babies, and discuss the changes in themselves, pointing out similarities and differences in the photographs. Later they use mirrors to look closely at their facial features before painting pictures of themselves. The student in the class uses some of the children's paintings, together with lots of open-ended questions to assess their observation skills.

TRY IT OUT

Take a group of children, between 3 and 4 years old, on a 'sound walk' and record what they can hear in pictorial form. For example:

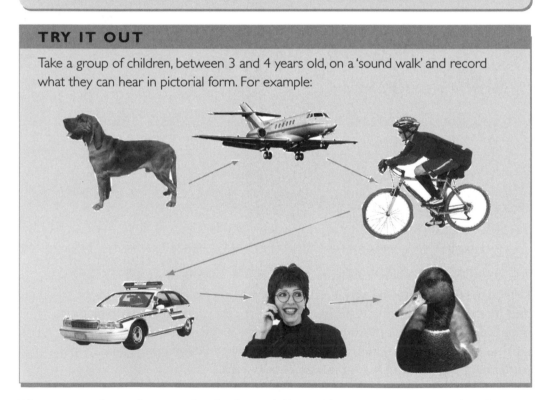

The picture above shows a dog barking, followed by an aeroplane overhead, a cyclist, a police car, someone talking on the phone, and a bird. Children can record the sounds as they walk or as they get back to the setting. This can be used as one observation to start assessing how children record information and use sensory awareness. The data can be used to plan appropriate activities in the future.

TRY IT OUT

◆ With parental permission record children talking about where they live, their environment and their families. Use this information, and the stepping stones, to plan future activities, but also to strengthen the partnership with parents. Think about the ideas of some researchers such as Bartholomew and Bruce (1993) who explain how parents cannot physically come into a setting, but can contribute to the observation process.

◆ Provide children with magnifying glasses and containers so that they can observe similarities and differences of man-made and natural objects. Use this observation to help you provide opportunities that extend the children's understanding of the world in which they live. Consider the curriculum approaches of Rudolph Steiner and Maria Montessori to help develop your understanding and knowledge of how to plan appropriate activities that meet the individual needs of children.

◆ Talk to the children about the changes in seasons. Use open-ended questions to help them develop prediction skills. Record their answers and use the data provided, and the stepping stones, to plan activities and experiences that will encourage the children to extend their prediction skills.

Practising balance and coordination plays an important role in physical development

Children do not make one observation as they explore the world around them, they make several, constantly readjusting their views and ideas as they observe and notice more. We should follow their example.

Remember, one observation is never sufficient evidence to fully and accurately assess a child's understanding, and in all cases more than one observation must be carried out in order to develop a holistic view of the child.

Physical development

This aspect of the foundation stage is about developing and extending the skills of coordination, control, balance, manipulation and movement. It also helps children gain confidence in their own abilities and allows them to feel the benefits of being active and healthy.

It can be very difficult to isolate one aspect of learning and development because children develop and learn holistically, and all areas of development are inter-related. However, it is possible to observe specific aspects of physical development through activities and experiences, such as kicking a football, using cutlery, fastening clothing, climbing, and riding a tricycle.

CASE STUDY

Angelina, aged three years and five months, is standing at the water tray. She is pouring water from a jug into different containers. Her key person observes that sometimes Angelina pours accurately and sometimes she spills water over the sides of the containers. The key person recognises that Angelina is developing control and hand-eye coordination, but is still not completely accurate. The key person makes a note to provide more opportunities that help Angelina develop accuracy, such as using sand instead of water and more play at the water tray. Also, the key person continues to praise Angelina's efforts at pouring to help her develop confidence in her own abilities.

TRY IT OUT

Plan an activity based on an obstacle course, providing children with opportunities to bend, stretch, climb over and through objects, move at different speeds, balance, and kick or throw soft balls. This can be set up both indoors or outside. Don't make this a competition between children, but praise their individual attempts and efforts to progress along the course. Try to record or make a note of parts of the course where some children struggle and then, using the observation and the stepping stones, plan specific activities and experiences to help them develop these skills.

You could also try one of the following points as an observation.

◆ Observe a group of children engaged in outdoor play using large pieces of equipment. Use the work of Margaret McMillan to help develop your understanding of firsthand learning and free play.

◆ Use stepping stones and developmental milestones or norms to help assess the observed development of a child that is using tools for a specific purpose, such as cutting by using scissors.

◆ Use an event sample to record how often a child takes a drink of water and in what context, such as after vigorous play. Again, the theories of McMillan may help extend your understanding of firsthand learning and free play. Consider how available water is to the children and if you need to provide more.

Young children grow and develop rapidly during the Foundation Stage. This includes developing control and coordination of their bodies and movement, and also confidence. Planned activities as a result of careful observations should provide opportunities for children to be active and challenged.

Creative development

Creative development is concerned with how children express their feelings, ideas and preferences using all of their senses. It can be improved in a wide variety of ways which include music, movement, opportunities to use imagination, communication, and children expressing themselves and their ideas. This area of learning is essential to successful and effective growth. Creativity enables children to make connections between the different areas of learning, and therefore make greater sense of their environment. Children need to feel secure and confident to try out different ways of doing things, and need to work at their own pace with time to think and plan. It is important to make them aware that creativity is not always spontaneous.

CASE STUDY

A group of children aged between three years six months and four years two months have watched a television programme about dinosaurs. After the programme Javid begins to paint a picture of a dinosaur, and his friend chooses to make a model using recycled materials. Other children start to make large, exaggerated movements and roar in imitation of the dinosaurs that they saw on the television. All of the children have responded in different creative ways to the programme.

TRY IT OUT

◆ Observe a child singing rhymes and familiar songs. Make a note of their facial expressions and body language, and their response to the music and rhythms. Look at the stepping stones for ways in which the adult could extend this aspect of development. You may find that the work of Vygotsky and scaffolding in the zone of proximal development could be helpful in extending your understanding and knowledge.

◆ The Waldorf/Steiner curriculum places a great deal of importance in aesthetic awareness. Observe a child painting freely and make notes of how they communicate their ideas and feelings. Use the ideas of Steiner and the stepping stones to develop your conclusion and evaluative sections of your observation. This observation also covers aspects of personal, social and emotional development and communication, language and literacy, and it could use a holistic approach to meeting the needs of the child.

◆ Observe children engaged in role-play. Research the ideas of Friedrich Froebel and his views on active learning through play. Use this information to extend and develop your observation.

While researching theoretical perspectives and theories it is also very important to keep abreast of current research and the latest views and opinions. For example, in November 2004 researchers from the Institute of Education, Birkbeck College, The University of London and Oxford University published their latest findings from the long-term study, Effective Provision of Pre-school Education (EPPE). This research shows that the earlier that children have access to high quality education, then the better they perform later in their school life. It was established that every month of pre-school education after the age of two was beneficial, and that disadvantaged children gain significant developmental benefits from attending pre-school, especially if they attend centres alongside children from different social backgrounds. Research of this nature is very important to all childcare and education professionals and has a direct impact on the provision offered during the foundation stage. It is crucial that the provision offered is of the best possible quality, giving children a full and rounded experience. Practitioners who are able to carry out sensitive observations and take a child's individual needs into consideration are the key to high quality provision.

Throughout this chapter, it has been repeatedly emphasised that one isolated observation is never enough, and that practitioners must carry out many observations of children. It is important to build up a holistic picture of the child's needs, achievements and development, because all areas impact on each other, for example, a language difficulty could affect a child's ability to make friends, develop relationships and even damage their confidence levels. Sensitive and thoughtful observations, underpinned by understanding and knowledge, are essential if practitioners are to be equipped to plan effective experiences and activities to support children's development and learning.

Chapter 8 Linking observations to the National Curriculum

Observation, as a means of assessing children's achievements, is not particularly common in schools offering the National Curriculum. This could be due to the fact that statutory assessment systems are in place. Observations are more often used to provide information of behavioural and emotional difficulties and other areas of concern such as child protection. However, some courses for practitioners working with the National Curriculum do include observations as part of the assessment process, for example the CACHE Level 3 Certificate for Teaching Assistants.

This chapter will consider:

◆ the structure of the National Curriculum with a brief overview

◆ how observations can support teachers and support staff in their assessment of children's progress

◆ the Numeracy and Literacy Strategies.

The structure of the National Curriculum

The National Curriculum is delivered to all children of compulsory school age in state schools throughout England and Wales. It became law in the Education Reform Act of 1988. Note that Scotland and Northern Ireland both have their own curriculum to ensure consistency of education during the compulsory school years. The National Curriculum does not apply to private schools, although many such establishments choose to follow it. The Education Reform Act of 1988 requires that all state schools provide children with a curriculum that is balanced and broadly based. The National Curriculum does not, however, constitute the whole curriculum for schools, because they have the discretion to develop a curriculum that reflects their particular needs and circumstances. There are strong links between the National Curriculum at Key Stage 1 and the Foundation Stage Curriculum.

The National Curriculum is organised into four key stages:

Key Stage 1 (KS1) – for children between five and seven years old (Infant Schools)

Key Stage 2 (KS2) – for children between seven and eleven years old (Junior Schools)

Key Stage 3 (KS3) – for children between eleven and fourteen years old (Secondary Schools)

Key Stage 4 (KS4) – for children between fourteen and sixteen years old (Secondary Schools)

Each key stage is divided into year groups:

◆ Reception being the end of the foundation stage

◆ Year 2 being the end of KS1

◆ Year 6 being the end of KS2

◆ Year 7 being the start of KS3

◆ Year 9 being the start of KS4, which ends at year 11 when children usually take GCSE examinations.

From the ages of five to eleven years all children study ten subjects – English, Maths, Science, Geography, History, Technology, Information Technology, Art, Music and Physical Education. Each subject has a programme of study that sets out the minimum knowledge, skills and understanding required at each key stage. At the end of each key stage there are descriptions which define the expected standards in each subject. These standards are assessed through attainment targets, or Standard Assessment Tests (SATs), and are recorded as a level. For example, a child could have achieved level 3 in Maths and Science and level 2 in English by the end of KS1. The attainment targets or levels allow an individual child's progress to be assessed and monitored throughout their school years.

Below is an extract from the KS1 in English, which can be accessed on the National Curriculum online website.

You are here: NC online > English > key stage 1 > En1 Speaking and listening

En1 Speaking and listening | **En2 Reading** | **En3 Writing**
Knowledge, skills and understanding

Speaking

1) To speak clearly, fluently and confidently to different people, pupils should be taught to:

    a. speak with clear diction and appropriate intonation
    b. choose words with precision
    c. organise what they say
    d. focus on the main point(s)
    e. include relevant detail
    f. take into account the needs of their listeners.

From eleven to sixteen children have more choice of subjects, such as foreign languages, food technology and many more. However, all children are expected to continue to study English, Maths and Science up to the end of Key Stage 4.

The table below is an extract from the KS3 in English.

You are here: NC online > English > key stage 3 > En1 Speaking and listening

En1 Speaking and listening | En2 Reading | En3 Writing
Knowledge, skills and understanding

Speaking

1) To speak fluently and appropriately in different contexts, adapting their talk for a range of purposes and audiences, including the more formal, pupils should be taught to:

   a. structure their talk clearly, using markers so that their listeners can follow the line of thought
   b. use illustrations, evidence and anecdote to enrich and explain their ideas
   c. use gesture, tone, pace and rhetorical devices for emphasis
   d. use visual aids and images to enhance communication
   e. vary word choices, including technical vocabulary, and sentence structure for different audiences
   f. use spoken **standard English** fluently in different contexts
   g. evaluate the effectiveness of their speech and consider how to adapt it to a range of situations.

At the end of each key stage children are assessed through SATs, except in Wales where children no longer have SATs at the end of Key Stage 1. Children following the National Curriculum in England and Wales take GCSE examinations at the end of Key Stage 4.

How observations can support assessment of progress

In September 2004 the way that children's progress is assessed at the end of Key Stage 1 changed from previous years. The emphasis is now on the teacher's judgement of a child's performance, which means that it should be easier to cater for individual and special needs. SATs at the end of Key Stage 1 will be more informal with teachers deciding on the most suitable time for the test to be carried out. This will mean that observations of children are crucial to providing accurate and sensitive assessments of children's progress and attainment.

Observations can inform teachers, classroom assistants and learning support assistants of a child's progress and attainment throughout the National Curriculum. Observations are an invaluable source of information and can be used to support children more effectively to meet their individual needs. Observations can be used to inform and support the planning process and to identify the individual learning needs of children. While quite common in KS1 and KS2, observations are not as widespread in KS3 and KS4, other than to provide evidence for other professionals regarding areas of concern or difficulty, however, the importance and value of observations at all stages of the National Curriculum should not be underestimated.

Many schools have developed proforma observation sheets to be used for each subject. This ensures consistency of approach and the information recorded throughout the school, and reduces the risk of the observer making judgemental statements or assumptions. Curriculum 2000 has recording sheets for all key stages to help adults record children's achievements and progress. An example is given below.

Science

Level 3

Comments/Evidence

Scientific Enquiry

▶▶▶

Responds to suggestions and puts forward own ideas about how to find the answer to a question.		
Recognises why it is important to collect data to answer questions.		
Uses simple texts to find information.		
Makes relevant observations and measures quantities, such as length or mass, using a range of simple equipment.		
Where appropriate carries out a fair test, with some help, recognising and explaining why it is fair.		
Records observations in a variety of ways.		
Provides explanations for observations and for simple patterns in recorded measurements.		
Communicates in a scientific way what they have found out and suggests improvements in their work.		
Entire Level Completed		

Sample recording sheet for Curriculum 2000

As mentioned in other chapters, one observation of a child is not enough to produce sufficient evidence. These recording sheets require frequent observations to be made of the children in order to complete the Comments/Evidence section on the right hand side.

CASE STUDY

Mandi is a learning support assistant in a large comprehensive school. She supports one 13 year old boy (year 9) in all subjects of the National Curriculum. He is at school action plus on the code of practice and has regular half termly reviews of his attainment and progress. The boy, his parents, form tutor, year group leader and Mandi are involved in the review process. To assist with the reviews Mandi undertakes weekly observations across all subject areas. Some of the observations, such as those in Maths, are in the form of a checklist to record specific skills and knowledge, whereas others are narrative/written accounts. Mandi also does event samples to record specific incidences of behaviour that cause concern and keeps a daily written diary that is shared with the parents.

Due to class size teachers often make observations without formally recording the data

Sometimes a specific observation may be required, such as when there is a cause for concern with behaviour, or a specific learning difficulty. In these circumstances the observer may use a technique other than a set proforma, such as written/narrative or event sample. Observations can also provide evidence which can be used by other professionals to support children in their learning, and possibly help identify areas of concern. Education psychologists will use observations that they, or others have made, as a diagnostic tool to help develop individual education plans (IEP).

Teachers make observations of children's progress almost instinctively, but may not formally record the data, frequently relying on their memory to retain information. Although this is understandable in a busy classroom and with the workload of teachers, it is not recommended because memories are not always reliable. For example, a teacher in a year 7 Textiles class observed that some of the children were having trouble threading a sewing machine. She made a mental note to revise this the following week. However, in the following week the main learning outcomes of the session did not include a revision on how to thread a sewing machine, so some children continued to struggle. If the teacher had recorded this information on the lesson plan, the revision of threading would have been included in the main learning outcomes.

TRY IT OUT

The opportunities to do observations within the National Curriculum are almost limitless. The following suggested observations for you to try will depend on your own personal work situation and may not therefore be possible for you to do. However, replace these suggestions with observations that are appropriate to your work situation and try to observe a range of subjects using different methods to record the information.

- Observe a child engaged in a Science activity at KS1, such as exploring and investigating familiar everyday objects. Use the National Curriculum level descriptors for Science to assess the child's attainment and suggest further activities to develop their knowledge and understanding.
- Observe a child in a Design and Technology lesson at KS3. Note how they approach the planning process. Use the National Curriculum for Design and Technology to assess the child's attainment and to recommend ways to support the child's progress.
- Observe a child in a History lesson at KS2, for example a topic on the Roman Invasion of Britain (this links into units 6a, 6b and 6c of the National Curriculum for History). Identify key words that are associated with this topic. Assess the child's understanding of these key words, can they spell them and use them in a correct context? You may, for example, wish to do this observation as a checklist with additional comments, or record their responses on tape.

The Numeracy and Literacy Strategies

As a result of a National Curriculum evaluation the National Literacy Strategy was introduced in 1998, followed by the National Numeracy Strategy in 1999. Both strategies have clear frameworks for teachers to follow and aim to increase standards in Literacy and Numeracy at key stages 1 and 2.

Classroom assistants and learning support staff are actively involved in planning and supporting teachers in the delivery of these strategies, and are also actively involved in the assessment of children's understanding and progress. It is regarded as good practice to encourage peer assessment, not just in activities associated with the National Numeracy and Literacy Strategies, but across the whole curriculum. This can provide very useful material to assist adults in assessing children's progress and attainment.

The Numeracy Strategy has four key principles:

◆ a dedicated maths lesson every day

◆ direct teaching and interactive oral work with groups and the whole class

◆ an emphasis on mental calculations

◆ controlled differentiation, with all children engaged in maths activities relating to a common theme.

Many schools refer to this strategy as the numeracy hour and plan these activities at the start of each school day. In reality the sessions last between 45 minutes and one hour and can be divided up as follows:

5–10 minutes on oral work and mental skills.

30–40 minutes on the main teaching activity, in groups, individually and whole class activities.

10–15 minutes on a plenary session with the whole class to sort out misconceptions, identify progress, summarise key facts and ideas, discuss the next steps and identify homework tasks.

Some schools deliver the numeracy hour as one full session while others divide it up into small chunks throughout the course of the school day.

The National Numeracy Strategy sets out the main objectives for each year group, some of which are more complicated than they initially seem and will involve children meeting teachers more than once in any school year. For example, choosing an appropriate operation to solve word problems will be revisited several times during KS2.

CASE STUDY

Sarah is a classroom assistant in a year 3 class. During the numeracy hour she works for short sessions with a group of five children who have difficulty reading, writing and ordering whole numbers up to 1000. The teacher and Sarah have planned and developed a series of graded worksheets to help support the children's learning. Sarah uses the worksheets together with question and answering techniques to observe and assess the children's progress before moving them on to the next stage.

TRY IT OUT

◆ Devise a checklist to record how children read, write and order whole numbers. Use the main objectives for your year group to define the highest number, for example 100, or 1000. Use the main learning objectives to measure a child's achievement and the evidence of the checklist to help you plan future activities for this child.

◆ Use children's work as observation evidence to assess their understanding of topics such as symmetry, fractions, money notation, and time.

◆ Observe a child who clearly needs support with mental work during a whole class activity. Using the evidence of your observation suggest activities and experiences that can help build the child's confidence in his/her abilities and make progress in this area. You may also want to link this observation to the work of Piaget on the stages of cognitive development.

THINK ABOUT IT

Jean Piaget believed that cognitive development occurred in stages and that development is a result of maturation and adaptation. Maturation is biological maturity and the environment has little impact on it. Adaptation is concerned with the environment and how the child is shaped by it. Piaget believed that each child had to pass through each stage, and none could be missed out. The stages are:

◆ sensori-motor stage from approximately 0–2 years

◆ pre-operational stage from approximately 2–7 years

◆ concrete operational stage from approximately 7–11 years

◆ formal operational stage from approximately 11 years.

Piaget believed that children need to be active learners and that the learning environment must be stimulating. It therefore follows that when Piaget's ideas are applied to the classroom the role of the adult is to provide opportunities that children can explore for themselves and can actively construct their own knowledge through appropriate activities and experiences.

Research Piaget's theory of cognitive development and that of other researchers, such as Donaldson, to extend your understanding of how children learn. Research the ideas of Vygotsky on how adults can support children's learning.

The National Literacy Strategy lessons are also designed to last approximately one hour. However, as with the Numeracy Strategy some schools deliver it in small portions throughout the day. It focuses on:

◆ phonics, spelling and vocabulary

◆ grammar and punctuation

◆ comprehension and composition.

This time can be divided up as follows:

15 minutes on whole class shared text work

15 minutes on whole class focused word work

20 minutes on group, individual work on reading and writing

10 minutes on plenary and evaluation of activities to identify progress, make links to other work, discuss the next steps and set homework.

Targets or main learning objectives are set in listening and speaking, reading and writing within each year group and these match the programmes of study for the National Curriculum in English.

CASE STUDY

Laura is a classroom assistant in a year 5 class. The whole class are looking at different kinds of poems and individual tasks have been set for the children to write their own poems in any form that they choose. They are actively encouraged to become involved in peer assessment, in which children comment constructively on each other's work. Laura listens to and records comments of two children assessing each other's work. The teacher and Laura use this observation to assess how the children have chosen their words and phrases in their poems to reflect their feelings and moods.

Some local education authorities have developed literacy programmes to support the National Literacy Strategy. For example, at Key Stage 1 some schools in Shropshire have piloted a phonics programme using puppets, stories and rhymes, on top of structured activities, to help children develop their reading skills. Often these sessions are led by specially trained classroom assistants, who work with small groups of children during the allocated literacy hour or at specific times during the day. The Shropshire programme includes checklists and charts for the adult to record achievement and attainment for each child following observations of the children.

TRY IT OUT

◆ Observe a child during the plenary session. Make a note of their involvement and responses. Use this information to help you assess how carefully the child has listened.

◆ Use an event sample to record how often children write for different purposes during the school day, such as messages, reports, letters, information and stories. Think about how you could assess this information using the level descriptors of the National Curriculum or the main learning objectives of the Literacy Strategy.

◆ Observe a child during a reading activity. Make a note of how the child responds to punctuation and the meaning of words.

The National Curriculum has been subject to significant modification in the 15 years since it was introduced. Some of the changes have been positive and some have been negative, often causing frustration for those trying to deliver it. Changes to the curriculum are often the result of pressure from particular lobby groups, for example the English curriculum now contains promotional material from 'all walks of life'. The curriculum should reflect the needs and values of society as addressed through legislation, for example, the present government gives higher priority to some aspects of education than others.

It is important for adults involved in delivering the National Curriculum to read the introductory sections for each subject, because these provide a rationale for the provision and delivery of the curriculum.

Glossary of key terms

Affect: to make something different, having an effect or influence on something

Aim: overall purpose, the main reason or point of something

Analysis: an examination or investigation of an idea, breaking something down into parts and then restructuring it

Aspect: one of the four sections of the Birth to Three Matters Framework

Assess: to go through the evidence, information and decide upon outcomes and conclusions

Assessment: a measurement or judgement of understanding, knowledge and skills

Authentic: original work

Behaviourism: learning as a result of activities and experiences shapes development

Bias: not a balanced comment or judgement, unfair or showing favouritism

Bibliography: a logical list of books, journals, articles, websites and other material that has been used when working on an observation, or other piece of work

Birth to Three Matters Framework: a framework to support those people working with and caring for babies and young children under three years old

CA: Classroom Assistant

Child Development: the study of how children grow, mature, learn and develop skills

Compare: look for and explain similarities and differences

Component: one of the sections of an aspect of the Birth to Three Matters Framework

Conclusion: summarise the findings of the observation

Confidentiality: maintaining and respecting the right to privacy of another individual

CTA: Classroom Teaching Assistant

Curriculum: a set of activities, experiences and opportunities that enable children to develop and learn

Echolalia: repeating single words or short phrases

Effect: the consequences or result of an action or activity/experience

ELG: Early Learning Goal (from the foundation stage)

EPPE: Effective Provision of Pre-school Education (a long term research project)

Evaluate/evaluation: an assessment of facts to indicate the value of something, or an aspect of development or theory

Explain: give details of something, to put into plain words

Foundation Stage Curriculum: a set of activities and experiences divided into six areas of learning for children between three and five years old

Heuristic play: play with natural materials that encourages and stimulates sensory development, particularly in babies

Holistic: all of the areas of child development

IEP: Individual Education Plan, can also be called and ILP (Individual Learning Plan)

Interpret: understand, clarify, or explain

IQ: Intelligence Quotient

Key person: a responsive, warm and sensitive adult with whom a baby or young child can form a secure attachment

KS: Key Stage (part of the National Curriculum)

LAD: Language Acquisition Device attributed to Chomsky

LSA: Learning Support Assistant

Legislation: laws that have been passed by parliament

Method: a way of doing something, a specific technique

National Curriculum: a set of learning activities and experiences for children between 5 and 16 years of age

Nature versus nurture: ongoing debate as to whether the environment and external factors (nurture) have a greater impact on development than genetically inherited traits (nature)

Needs: essential requirements that a child must have in order to develop, grow and learn

Normative assessment: assessment of development or learning using norms

Pincer grasp: using the index finger and thumb to pick up or grasp an object

Palmar grasp: using the whole hand to pick up or grasp an object

Plagiarism: copying the work of another person and passing it off as your own

Portage: a home-based specialised curriculum to meet the individual needs of children who have special educational needs

Predict: forecast, or to think ahead

Primary carer: the adult who has the main responsibility for caring for a child, such as a parent, close relative, foster parent or childcare and education worker

Profile: usually a record of a child's achievements

Proforma: a prepared chart or table used to record observation evidence

Objective: a specific, measurable goal or target

QCA: qualifications and Curriculum Authority

Rationale: several reasons or ideas that have a common link or theme, an underlying principle

Recommendation: sensitive, appropriate and relevant suggestion about the subject to promote development and improve practice

Reference: the acknowledged use of someone else's work to support your own views and findings

SATs: Standard Assessment Tests

Schema: an early concept or idea based on linked patterns of behaviour; originally attributed to Piaget

Sociogram: an observational technique used to collect evidence of social interactions within a group of children

Statutory: has been made legal

Stepping stones: progressive stages of achievement within each area of learning in the Foundation Stage

Strategies: ways of doing something

Telegraphic speech/Telegraphese: using two word phrases to express meaning

Theory: a well researched and unique idea or perspective on a particular subject or topic

Theorist: an individual who has extensively researched a subject or topic and produced a unique and original view

ZPD: zone of proximal development attributed to Vygotsky

Table of researchers, theorists and theoretical perspectives

Please note that this table is not a definitive list and apologies go to any current researchers who have not been included.

Name	Dates (if applicable)	Main area of study	Main features
Lesley Abbott	Current researcher	Early years curriculum, play and Birth to Three Matters Framework	Play promotes learning. Led the team that developed the Birth to Three Matters Framework
Mary Ainsworth	Current researcher	Attachment	Developed the work of Bowlby and separation anxiety
Chris Athey	Current researcher	Cognitive development	Developed and researched the concept of schemas
Albert Bandura	1925–	Social learning	Studied how children learn from role models and how this can influence their learning and behaviours
Alfred Binet	1857–1911	Measurement of intelligence	Developed a series of tasks to measure intelligence in both adults and children
Peter Blos	Current researcher	Development of adolescent identity	Friend of Erikson, adolescence is an important time for reducing the impact of earlier negative events
John Bowlby	1907–1990	Attachment	Looked at the effects of forming strong bonds and attachments, usually with a maternal figure.
Tina Bruce	Current researcher	Early Years Education and Play	Considers the value of play in early years education, introduced the idea of freeflow play

Name	Dates (if applicable)	Main area of study	Main features
Jerome Bruner	1915–	Scaffolding	Built on the beliefs of Vygotsky but developed the idea that children develop different ways of thinking rather than passing through stages. Considered the role of the adult in helping children learn
Robert Case	Current Researcher	Cognitive development	Believes cognitive development is based on information processing theory
Noam Chomsky	1928–	Language development	Introduced the idea of a language acquisition device (LAD) which was instinctive. Can be linked to the nature/nurture debate
A.D.B & A.M. Clark	Current researchers	Early years experiences	How early experiences can affect but not necessarily determine later development
V Das Gupta	Current researcher	Cognitive and language development	Developing the theories of Piaget and Vygotsky
Margaret Donaldson	1926–	Cognitive development – how children think	Built on the work of Piaget, well-known for her book 'Children's Minds'
Judy Dunn	Current Researcher	Language Development	Concept of causal talk and the notion of the concept of cause
Erik Erikson	1902–1939	Emotional and personality development	A student of Freud; felt that emotional and social development are linked to cognitive and language development. Personality continues to develop into adulthood. Stages of development are called psychosocial as children explore relationships
Jerry Fodor	Current researcher	Cognitive development	Believes that all children are born with identical representational systems that are genetically structured to allow us to make sense of the world

Name	Dates (if applicable)	Main area of study	Main features
Sigmund Freud	1856–1939	Emotional and personality development	First theorist to consider the unconscious mind and its effects on development. Believed development was stage-like; stages are called psychosexual and are linked to the physical pleasures associated with each stage.
Fredrich Froebel	1782–1852	Early learning through play	Established the first Kindergarten, believed in indoor and outdoor play and placed great value on symbolic behaviour
H Gardener	Current researcher	Multiple intelligences	Worked on genetically determined mental operations
Arnold Gesell	1880–1961	Maturation	Described patterns of development that are genetically programmed
William Glasser	1925–	Needs	Believed in empowering children through non-judgemental recognition leading to a positive feeling of self-worth
Eleanor Goldschmeid	Current researcher	Heuristic play and the role of the key person	Influenced by the views of Piaget, heuristic play stimulates physical and cognitive development. Considered the need for children to have secure relationships with a key person
Florence Goodenough	1886–1959	Drawings as a measure of intelligence	Developed the 'Draw a Man' test with point scoring system
Penny Holland	Current researcher	Physical play, superhero play and war games	Researched the effect of a zero tolerance policy on children's development
Michael Howe	Current researcher	Intelligence	Emphasises the role of the environment in changing children's IQ

Name	Dates (if applicable)	Main area of study	Main features
Susan Isaacs	1885–1948	Value of play and the role of parents	Influenced by Froebel. Believed that play would enable children to have a balanced view of life, and that parents are the main educators of children
A Karmiloff-Smith	Current researcher	Language development	Proposed that babies are born with a number of domain-specific constraints which help give the child a positive start to life
Lawrence Kohlberg	1927–1987	Moral development and gender identity	Extended and redefined Piaget's views. Suggested that individuals develop moral reasoning in six stages and three levels. Sex roles emerge as stage-like development in cognition
John Locke	1632–1704	Education	Believed that babies are born with everything to learn, 'an empty vessel'
Abraham Maslow	1908–1970	Needs	Developed a hierarchy of needs that follow the life cycle. The hierarchy has five levels and is dynamic, with the dominant need always shifting
Margaret McMillan	1860–1931	First-hand learning, importance of health and social education and free play	Member of the Froebel Society. Believed in training for early years workers. Established the first open air nursery
Maria Montessori	1870–1952	Structured play	Believed children have times in their lives when they are more able to learn certain things than at other times
Robert Owen	1771–1858	Early education	Believed that the educational environment was a prime factor in shaping children's learning, social development and behaviour

Name	Dates (if applicable)	Main area of study	Main features
Ivan Pavlov	1849–1980	Classical conditioning	Studied a type pf learning where an automatic response such as a reflex is triggered by a new stimulus. Worked primarily with dogs
Jean Piaget	1896–1980	Cognitive and language development, also play and moral understanding	Introduced the theory of stages of cognitive development, considered how children learn concepts. Also considered stages of play and moral development. Highly influential
Robert Plomin	Current Researcher	Genetic influences on development	Recognition of the importance of genetic influences on individual differences between people, adopted children and their families
Carl Rogers	1902–1987	Self-concept development	If the image of ourselves and the image of our ideal self are the same we will develop good self-esteem
H Schaffer	Current researcher	Social development	Social development and aspects of attachment
Selleck	Current researcher	Emotional and social development	The role of the key person and the need to establish secure relationships
Mary Sheridan	Current researcher	Physical development	Established developmental norms through repeated and numerous observations of children
B.F. Skinner	1904–1990	Behaviourist theory	Worked primarily with animals, remembered for the 'Skinner box' and introduced the idea that a behaviour would be repeated if reinforced
Rudolf Steiner	1861–1925	Community Education	Believed relationships between children and adults are very important if a child is to develop to their full potential

Name	Dates (if applicable)	Main area of study	Main features
Edward Thorndike	1874–1949	Reinforcement	Followed on from the work of Skinner. Assumed that learning happens due to an association being made between a stimulus and a response and the pleasure/satisfaction that follows
Lev Vygotsky	1896–1934	Social learning	Worked along similar lines to Piaget in that he believed children are active learners, but also upheld that social development is a very important part of cognitive development. Introduced the idea of the zone of proximal development (ZPD)

Table of developmental norms

While developmental norms or milestones are useful indicators of a child's development it is important to remember that every child is unique. They will develop at different rates according to their individual experiences, activities, the environment in which they live and the other people with whom they interact.

All areas of development are inter-related and it is often difficult to look at just one area, especially in relation to assessing progress and achievement. Focusing on only one area of development may prevent the observer from considering other important factors that are not necessarily part of that specific area. For example, a language difficulty can lead to frustration (related to emotional development) and difficulties communicating with peers (related to social skills). A holistic approach will give a better insight into the needs of the child and enable the practitioner to plan and provide appropriate experiences and activities.

This table is presented as guidance only and readers are advised not to make assumptions about a child's development. The ages given are rough guides to stages of development.

Approximate age	Physical development	Theoretical perspective or theory to consider if relevant
Newborn	Primitive reflexes should be present. Moves legs less often than arms. Sucks vigorously. Sleeps for about 21 out of 24 hours, not awake for very long.	**Birth to Three Matters** – a framework to support practice from birth to three years **Piaget** – sensori-motor stage of development
Six weeks	Can lift head. Will follow a moving object with eyes for a few seconds. Looks into space when awake. Limb movements still uncoordinated. Still spends most of the time asleep or drowsing.	**Mary Sheridan** – developmental norms

Approximate age	Physical development	Theoretical perspective or theory to consider if relevant
Three to five months	Waves arms in controlled manner. Kicks and pushes feet against a firm surface. Can roll from back to side. Can hold head steadily. Watches hands and fingers, clasps hands. When lying on stomach can lift head and pushes upwards with arms. Sleeps for about 16 hours a day.	
Six to eight months	Can sit with support for long periods and for short periods without support. Can grasp using whole hand, (palmar grasp). Takes every object to the mouth. Arms move purposefully. Can roll from back to stomach. Can pull themselves into a standing position if helped. Hands and eyes are coordinated. First tooth may appear. Practices making different sounds.	**Lesley Abbott** – play throughout all ages **Tina Bruce** – play throughout all ages **A.D.B & A.M. Clark** – early experiences **Fredrich Froebel** – early experiences through play
Nine to eleven months	Very active, rolls and wriggles, begins to crawl or shuffle. Can reach sitting position without help. Can pick up objects with first finger and thumb (pincer grasp). Handles everything within reach, can pass objects from one hand to the other and carry them to the mouth. Top lateral incisors may appear. Sleeps about 14 hours a day.	**Eleanor Goldschmeid** – heuristic play and sensory development **Susan Isaacs** – play **Margaret McMillan** – importance of the outdoors and play

Approximate age	Physical development	Theoretical perspective or theory to consider if relevant
Twelve to fourteen months	Can pull themselves into a standing position. May walk around furniture. May walk with adult support or independently. Can crawl or shuffle very quickly. Can hold a cup. Points and can put small objects into a container. Uses hands and eyes to explore objects rather than mouth.	**Maria Montessori** – structured play
Fifteen to seventeen months	Restless and active. Stands alone. Can walk unaided. Can kneel. Can go upstairs on hands and knees. Can build a tower of two blocks. Can make marks with crayons. Can feed themselves with finger foods, tries to use spoon.	
Eighteen to twenty one months	Walks fairly well, can push and pull toys when walking, can walk backwards. Can come downstairs with adult help. Squats and bends from waist to pick up objects. Canine teeth may erupt.	

Approximate age	Physical development	Theoretical perspective or theory to consider if relevant
Two years	Can run, kick a ball from a standing position, climbs on furniture. Uses a spoon to feed themselves. Can zip and unzip large zippers. Can draw circles and dots. Will build a tower of five or six bricks. Begins to use a preferred hand. Begins to develop bowel and bladder control. By the end of the third year usually has a full set of milk teeth.	Penny Holland – physical play, superhero play and war games
Three years	Walks and runs with confidence, can walk on tiptoes, can throw and kick a ball. Jumps off low steps. Can pedal and steer a tricycle. Washes and dries hands with help. Can put on and take off some items of clothing independently. Turns pages in a book independently. Can use scissors.	Foundation Stage
Four years	Can walk on a line, hop on one foot. Bounces and catches a large ball. Runs changing direction. Buttons and unbuttons own clothing. Can cut out simple shapes.	
Five years	Skips with a rope. Can form letters, writes own name. Dresses and undresses independently. Can complete a 20 piece jigsaw. Can hit a ball with a bat. Begins to lose milk teeth.	National Curriculum

Approximate age	Physical development	Theoretical perspective or theory to consider if relevant
Six to seven years	Active and energetic. Enjoys using large apparatus. Moves to music with understanding. Can ride a bicycle without stabilisers. Hops, skips and jumps with confidence. Kicks a ball with direction. Balances on a beam or wall. Handwriting is evenly spaced.	
Eight to eleven years	Greater agility and control. All physical activities carried out with poise, coordination and precision. General health is usually good, appetite is good and food is enjoyed. Energy levels can suddenly drop so may need a short rest and food, but usually recovers quickly.	

Approximate age	Cognitive and language development	Theoretical perspective or theory to consider if relevant
Newborn	Conscious of and will respond to changes in temperature, some sounds, bright lights and contact with another human. Appears to copy facial expressions of other adults. Are egocentric.	**Birth to Three Matters** **Piaget** – sensori–motor development **Donaldson** – development of thought and language **Chomsky** – language acquisition device **Athey** – schemas **Bruner** – theory of cognitive development

Approximate age	Cognitive and language development	Theoretical perspective or theory to consider if relevant
Six weeks	Cries to communicate needs e.g. hunger, distress, tiredness. Recognises and responds to primary carer's voice. Learning about the world through the senses.	**Vygotsky** – ZPD **Bandura** – social learning
Three to five months	Smiles in response to other faces. More alert and interested in surroundings. Soothed by sound of carer's voice. Begins to make cooing and babbling noises.	**Jerry Fodor** – cognitive development **Bruner** – development of learning **Pavlov** – classical conditioning **Skinner** – operant conditioning **Thorndike** – reinforcement **Robert Case** – cognitive development **V Das Gupta** cognitive and language development
Six to eight months	Laughs, squeals with delight and chuckles. Babbles short sounds such as ma, ma, ma, da, da, da. Begins to develop object permanence. Learns mainly from trial and error.	**Dunn** – language development

Approximate age	Cognitive and language development	Theoretical perspective or theory to consider if relevant
Nine to eleven months	Babbling is the predominant sound, made up of non-crying sounds. Becomes more 'melodic' and has some 'intonation'. Includes all sounds needed for the language being learnt. Strings vowels and consonants together. Use gestures such as pointing to communicate needs. Can understand roughly seventeen words by eleven months. Can find an object that has been hidden. Enjoys and will respond to rhymes and finger play.	**H Gardener** – cognitive development **Michael Howe** – cognitive development **A. Karmiloff–Smith** – language development
Twelve to fourteen months	First words appear. One word can mean more than one thing depending on the tone of voice used – holophrases. Begins to scribble.	
Fifteen to seventeen months	Usually has about ten recognisable words. Can point to a named picture. May point to parts of the body.	
Eighteen to twenty three months	Two words put together. Emergence of telegraphic speech. Can learn between 10 and 30 new words in a month. Telegraphic speech emerges. Emergence of animism.	
Two years	Uses plurals, but can make grammatical errors, e.g. mousse. Starts to use questions and negatives. Vocabulary rapidly increases. Can complete a three piece puzzle. Can match three colours. Can stack in order. Pre-operational stage.	

Approximate age	Cognitive and language development	Theoretical perspective or theory to consider if relevant
Three years	Imitates speech of adults. Speech usually understood by strangers. Knows and understands nursery rhymes. Enjoys asking questions. Knows the difference between sizes such as big and little.	Foundation Stage
Four years	Language is developed and refined. Can repeat a simple story. Matches one to one. Knows primary colours. Can name at least three shapes. Can count up to 10.	
Five years	Vocabulary can be about 5000 words. Counts up to 20 by rote. Usually can name eight colours. Can match symbol.	National Curriculum
Six to seven years	Enjoys hearing and telling jokes. Uses complex sentences correctly. Begins to read with confidence. Can count up to 100 by rote. Can predict. Can arrange objects in order. Can name days of the week. Beginning of concrete operational stage. Can decentre and conserve.	

Approximate age	Cognitive and language development	Theoretical perspective or theory to consider if relevant
Eight to eleven years	Speaking, writing and reading are usually fluent. Understands the different uses of language. Handwriting is usually well formed and shows competence. Formal operation stage may emerge towards eleven years. Logical and methodical when problem solving, may not always use trial and error.	

Approximate age	Emotional and social development	Theoretical perspective or theory to consider if relevant
Newborn	Seems most contented when in close contact with mother/primary carer. Need to develop a strong bond or attachment with carers.	**Mary Ainsworth** – attachment
Six weeks	Seems to sense presence of mother/primary carer. Responds to human voice. Watches primary carer's face. Can swing rapidly from pleasure to unhappiness.	**John Bowlby** –attachment **Abraham Maslow** – needs **William Glasser** – needs
Three to five months	Smiles and shows pleasure. Enjoys being held and cuddled. Still has rapid mood swings.	**Erik Erikson** – stages of development **Eleanor Goldschmeid** – role of the key worker/person **Selleck** – role of the key worker/person

Approximate age	Emotional and social development	Theoretical perspective or theory to consider if relevant
Six to eight months	May show anxiety towards strangers. Eager and interested in everything going on around them. Laughs, chuckles and vocalises when with mother or familiar people, generally friendly. Shows anger when a plaything is removed, but easily distracted.	**H Schaffer** – social development and attachment
Nine to eleven months	Can distinguish between familiar people and strangers. Will show annoyance and anger through body movements such as kicking legs. Begins to play peek-a-boo games. Begins to wait for attention.	**Sigmund Freud** – personality development
Twelve to fourteen months	Affectionate towards members of the family and primary carers. Plays simple games. Growing independence can lead to rage when thwarted. Mood swings less violent. Shows little fear and much curiosity.	**Lawrence Kohlberg** – gender identity and moral reasoning
Fifteen to seventeen months	Emotionally more unstable than at one year. Can show jealously. Swings from being independent to dependent on an adult. Has more sense of being an individual.	**Piaget** – moral reasoning
Eighteen to twenty one months	Can be obstinate and unwilling to follow adult suggestions. Very curious, but short attention span. Mood swings.	**Carl Rogers** – development of self concept

Approximate age	Emotional and social development	Theoretical perspective or theory to consider if relevant
Two years	Shows self-will and may have tantrums, nightmares and irrational fears. Tries to be independent. Has strong emotions. Copies adult activities and actions. Parallel play and begins to engage in pretend play.	
Three years	Becomes more cooperative, adopts attitudes and moods of adults. Wants adult approval. Asks lots of questions. Shows concern for others. Begins to share playthings.	Foundation Stage
Four years	Confident, shows purpose and persistence. Shows control over emotions. Has adopted standards of behaviour of parents, family members. Develops friendships with peers.	B.F. Skinner – behaviour theory
Five years	Self-confident Shows desire to do well and will persevere at a new task. Still seeks adult approval. Shows good control of emotions. Cooperative play with both boys and girls, usually has a best friend. Enjoys stories of strong people.	National Curriculum
Six to seven years	Emotions can be more unstable than at five years, can be moody. Independent and may be solitary for short periods. Father's or male authority not usually questioned. Teacher's standards often accepted over mother's.	

Approximate age	Emotional and social development	Theoretical perspective or theory to consider if relevant
Eight to eleven years	Emotionally independent of adults. Need to be accepted by peers. Usually good control of emotions. Intolerant of weak adults. Enjoys team games. Towards the end of this period sexes begin to socialise separately.	Abraham Maslow – needs

References, bibliography and further reading

Athey C. (1990) *Extending Thought in Young Children*, Paul Chapman Publishing

Barnard H. C. (1969) *A History of English Education*, University of London Press

Bruce T. (1997) *Early Childhood Education (2nd edition)*, Hodder & Stoughton

Davenport G. C. (1993) *An Introduction to Child Development*, Collins Educational

Donaldson M. (1978) *Children's Minds*, Fontana Press

Dunn J. (1993) *Young Children's Close Relationships*, Sage Publications

Fawcett M. (1996) *Learning Through Child Observation*, Jessica Kingsley Publishers

Flanagan C. (1996) *Applying Psychology to Early Child Development*, Hodder and Stoughton

Gussin Paley V. (1990) *The Boy Who Would Be a Helicopter*, Harvard University Press

Holland P. (2003) *We don't play with guns here*, Open University Press

Kamen T. (2000) *Psychology for Childhood Studies*, Hodder & Stoughton

Oates J. (1994) *The Foundations of Child Development*, Blackwell

Sutherland P. (1992) *Cognitive Development Today – Piaget and his Critics*, Paul Chapman Publishing

Wells G. (1986) *The Meaning Makers*, Hodder & Stoughton

Bakhurst D. & Shanker S. G. (2001) *Jerome Bruner: Language, Culture, Self*, Sage Publications

Barratt-Pugh C. & Rohl M. (Ed) (2000) *Literacy Learning in the Early Years*, Open University Press

Drummond, M. J. et al (1992) *Making Assessment Work, Values and Principles in Assessing Young Children's Learning*, London NES Arnold, in association with the National Children's Bureau

Grieve R. & Hughes M. (1990) *Understanding Children,* Blackwell

Jarvis M. & Chandler E. (2001) *Angles on Child Psychology,* Nelson Thornes

Lee V. & Gupta P. D. (1995) *Children's Cognitive and Language Development,* Blackwell

Sharman C., Cross W. & Vennis D. (2002, 2nd edition) *Observing Children,* Continuum

Tizard B. & Hughes M. (2002) *Young Children Learning (2nd edition),* Blackwell

Tryphon A. & Vonèche J. (1996) *Piaget–Vygotsky – The Social Genesis of Thought,* Psychology Press

Curriculum Guidance for the Foundation Stage (2000), QCA

Nursery World, 26 September 2002

Nursery World, 6 February 2003

www.ibs.derby.ac.uk

www.connect.net

www.infed.org

www.utm.edu/research

www.users.globalnet.co.uk

References, bibliography and further reading

Index